Sussex Women

Women

Famous Infamous Unsung

Written and Compiled
by
Sharon Searle

Sharon Searle 2003

Introduction
by
Jasper Ridley

S.B. Publications
in association
with the author

First published by JAK Books 1995
PO Box 275, Tunbridge Wells, Kent TN4 0YH

Revised edition published in 2002 by S.B. Publications
in association with the author, Sharon Searle.
c/o 19 Grove Road, Seaford, East Sussex BN25 1TP.

ISBN: 1 85770 260 3

Typeset and Printed by Pageturn Ltd, East Sussex, BN3 7EG. Tel: 01273 821500

Front Cover Illustrations:
Top: Lee Miller   *Centre left:* Vera Pragnell
Centre right: Milly Dayrell   *Bottom:* Lady Anne Blunt

Back Cover Illustrations:
Main: Sheila Kaye-Smith   *Top Right:* Dame Grace Kimmins   *Bottom:* Julie Tullis

To Pim -
who first taught me to love the written word

ACKNOWLEDGEMENTS

I am greatly indebted to all the people who have helped me during the preparation of this book. Some have verified details, some have suggested further sources of information, others have brought to my attention women of Sussex I hadn't previously encountered.

In particular I wish to thank Dr Michael Ashby FRCP, Bowen Aylmer-Pearse, Hugh and Martine Bailey, David Burrough, Eileen Burrough, Joy Charlesworth, Kitty Graveley, Stephanie Green, Verena Hambury, Martin Hayes, Mary Hillyar, Rosalind Hodge, Robin Knibb, Bernie Lane, Jose and Edward Loosemore, Chris McCooey, Anthony Penrose, Hylda Rawlings,
Elsie Stuart, Terry Tullis, and Sister Winifred of The Society of the Holy Child Jesus.

I must also express my deep gratitude for the help given by Danehill Parish Historical Society, Pevensey Historical Society, the Sussex Archaeological Society and the County Records Office.

At some point during the last year, I have visited nearly every library in Sussex. All were helpful, but I particularly wish to mention the libraries of Brighton, Crawley, Crowborough, Eastbourne, Hailsham, Hove, Lewes, Polegate and Worthing.

Bryan Darby should have his own line – his help on the computer side has been invaluable.

My special thanks to Jasper Ridley and Kathleen Strange for reading the typescript. They made many useful suggestions.

I also wish to thank my family and friends for their support, encouragement – and patience.

Sharon Searle

CONTENTS

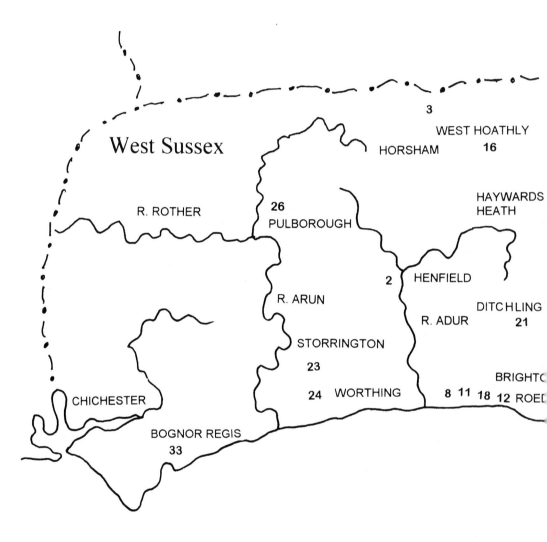

West Sussex

R. ROTHER

HORSHAM

WEST HOATHLY
16

3

HAYWARDS
HEATH

26
PULBOROUGH

R. ARUN

2

HENFIELD

DITCHLING
21

R. ADUR

STORRINGTON

23

CHICHESTER

24   WORTHING

8 11 18 12 ROEC

BRIGHTC

BOGNOR REGIS
33

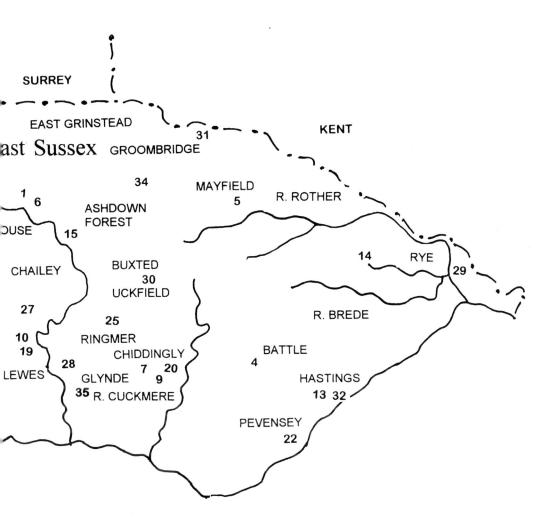

SURREY

EAST GRINSTEAD

ast Sussex GROOMBRIDGE

31

KENT

34

MAYFIELD

R. ROTHER

1

6

5

ASHDOWN
FOREST

OUSE

15

14

RYE

29

CHAILEY

BUXTED

30

UCKFIELD

R. BREDE

27

25

10

RINGMER

19

CHIDDINGLY

BATTLE

28

7

20

4

LEWES

GLYNDE

9

HASTINGS

35

R. CUCKMERE

13 32

PEVENSEY

22

PERSONAL NOTE

Right at the start, I'd better come clean and confess that I'm not a historian. My secondary school history teacher's idea of igniting interest in the past was to fill three blackboards with dates at the beginning of each year. The dates were wiped off at the end of the year after successive classes had spent three terms reciting in unison the bare facts of the relevant historical events until all but brain-dead.

I have, however, written a number of local history articles and while rooting around Sussex over the years, have come across some fascinating historical characters. I found the women particularly interesting, partly because, in comparison with the men, they come to light so infrequently. But when they do come to light, they shine.

The almost insurmountable problem of a book on Sussex women is who to include and who to leave out. Three women had to be included, because it was they who sparked off the original idea. Initially, I had learned the story of Cornelia Connelly who, despite being a woman of great intellect and energy, totally subjugated her personal needs for the sake of her faith. Almost immediately afterwards, I was told the stories of Marie Corbett and her jodhpurs, and Margery Corbett Ashby in Turkey – a mother and daughter who literally changed the world around them.

Some of the women were born here, others adopted the county, all affected Sussex in some way. The subtitle, Famous, Infamous, Unsung, is only a general description and some of the women fall into more than one category. Some women are noticeable for their absence. Katherine Howard, Mrs Fitzherbert and Virginia Woolf have already had enough written about them and this book is for the women of Sussex who are in danger of being forgotten.

And so, to come to the reasons why these particular women are included. They all have two things in common. The first is that they had a particular driving force in their lives. With some it was a compulsion which inspired them to change the world, with others it was a simple determination to survive. This force could also be called love – for another person or for mankind, for property, possessions or achievement – in most cases it was used for good, but not always. The second thing these women of Sussex have in common, is that every one of their stories made me raise my eyebrows at least once.

Sharon Searle, June 1995.

INTRODUCTION

by Jasper Ridley

This book tells the stories of 41 Women of Sussex who deserve to be better remembered than they are. Some of'them were famous in their day, but have been all but forgotten. Only the older generation remember the acting ability of Nancy Price. Even the best-selling novelist of the 1920s, Sheila Kaye-Smith, is largely forgotten; and hardly anyone has heard of Margaret Fairless Barber, whose book *The Roadmender* sold 250,000 copies in 1900, or the successful 18th century writer, Charlotte Smith. There are also women who were never famous, and did not wish to be.

Some of them founded churches and schools, or saved children from the workhouse. Grace Kimmins founded Chailey Heritage. Mabel Raymonde-Hawkins founded an animal sanctuary and Vera Pragnell one for human beings. The Lawrence sisters opened a public school for girls at Roedean. Viscountess Wolseley founded Glynde College for Lady Gardeners Charlotte King produced Greek plays for the villagers in West Hoathly, and Lady Wentworth bred Arab horses.

There are brave adventurers as well as capable organisers. Julie Tullis, who knew the risks she was taking, stood on the summit of K2 before dying on the way down. Mary Wheatland saved lives at Bognor. Phoebe Hessel enlisted as a soldier to follow her true love to the wars, and must surely have inspired the famous song *Polly Oliver*. Lady Pelham defended her husband's castle at Pevensey in 1399: and the beautiful American, Lee Miller – a war correspondent in the Second World War.

There are the champions of women's rights and liberal causes, Barbara Bodichon, Sophia Jex-Blake, and Margery Corbett Ashby; Barbara Willard of Ashdown Forest; Mrs Steere and Miss Rickman, grave-diggers of Lewes; Martha Gunn and her bathing machines at Brighton and Cornelia Connelly, who sacrificed her personal happiness for the Catholic Church and her religious society, and who is already on the way to being canonised. There is the Duchess of Leinster, the motor mechanic's daughter who married a duke and spent her life avoiding creditors; two women falsely accused of witchcraft in 17th century Rye; two murderers, Christiana Edmunds and Sarah Ann French; and the ghost of Nan Tuck, disappearing into thin air in the dark woods near Buxted.

Some of these women excite our admiration, others our pity, and some both our admiration and our pity. They have one thing in common: they were all unusual and remarkable women, whose life stories will interest many readers, and especially those who live in Sussex.

DAME MARGERY CORBETT ASHBY
(1882-1981)
SUFFRAGIST *NOT* SUFFRAGETTE

In 1972, Dame Margery Corbett Ashby spoke at the first public meeting of the Danehill Parish Historical Society. After the meeting, she was asked to become their first President – a position she accepted with enthusiasm. Five years later, she gave another talk to the Society on aspects of rural life in Victorian times as seen through the eyes of a squire's daughter. She spoke unhesitatingly for half an hour and spent another fifty minutes answering questions. An exceptional performance from a woman who was then 95 years old.

Looking at her family background, it is hardly surprising that Dame Margery was an exceptional woman. She was born in 1882 in the house called Woodgate at Danehill. Her father was a gifted barrister who held a deep concern for social and moral welfare. Her mother was Marie Corbett, a woman whose life and inspirational work with deprived children is described in another section of this book. Margery was educated at home, alongside her brother and sister. With her father, she

1

studied the classics, history and maths, with her mother, scripture and the piano. Governesses taught French and German and nurtured a talent which later made Margery a skilled linguist speaking Italian and Turkish and acting as translator at international conferences.

Woodgate was a home that frequently rang with laughter and music. The children had some extraordinary pets: squirrels, a badger rescued after its mother had been shot, a favourite pig that warmed its tummy in front of the fire. Margery's father brought a bantam cockerel home on the train one day, to the amusement of his fellow first class travellers.

When the time came to go to university, Margery took up a place at Newnham College, Cambridge, reading Classics. She immediately immersed herself in the work – not always Greek verse. A natural leader, she was soon heading a deputation to the College Principal to ask if it was really necessary to serve stewed prunes four times a week. Woodgate was renowned for its social functions and it was at a ball that Margery met the man who was to become her husband. Arthur Brian Ashby was a barrister and friend of her brother from New College, Oxford, and he fell in love with her at first sight. Determined to see her again, he left his gold watch behind after the ball so that he would have an excuse to come back.

They were engaged for five years before they could afford to marry, but they eventually set up home in a small house in Putney. Margery's interest in politics had always been encouraged by her Liberal parents and, inspired by her mother, she willingly became caught up in the women's rights movement. At the age of 16, she made her first political speech and at 19, she became national secretary of the Constitutional Suffrage Movement, a position she held for a year before becoming a member of the National Committee. As the Movement grew, militant suffragettes were chaining themselves to railings and posting burning oil rags through letter-boxes, but Margery thought of herself as a Suffragist not a Suffragette. Her father had told her that if you dress nicely and speak politely you will get most things you want in life.

"I talked to Mrs Pankhurst and to her daughter, Sylvia," she said, "and I admired their wonderful courage, but when they started hurting other people, I had to decide whether I wanted to go on working with the constitutional movement, or whether I would join the militants. Eventually, I decided that although I believed in the equality of men and women, there was one sphere in which there was no comparison and that was in sheer physical strength, so I remained a constitutional."

In 1904, she accompanied her mother to the first International Suffrage Congress in Berlin and, in 1907, she became Organising Secretary of the National Union of Women's Suffrage Societies. As a representative of the International Alliance of Women, she attended the Peace Conference at

Versailles and the International Labour Organisation and was instrumental in securing equality of the sexes within their constitutions. In 1920, she was elected secretary of the Alliance and in 1923, she became President.

Having lived through the First World War, Margery was active in the peace movement and was on the Executive Committee of the League of Nations Union. She took part in a campaign during which she spoke at meetings up and down the country.

"We had tremendous hopes that the League of Nations really would keep the peace," she said, ". . .I think it very nearly came off."

She remembered packed meetings, but also that sometimes stones were thrown and rats let loose.

"Of course," she commented, "being a countrywoman, I knew the rats were much more frightened of us than we were of them."

In 1932, she was a British delegate to the disarmament conference in Geneva, but she found it a deeply frustrating experience and later described her time there as dark days. After the Second World War, she resigned her post with the Alliance, but continued to travel extensively, lecturing in 27 different countries as a pacifist and for women's rights.

Possibly her least known, but single greatest triumph occurred in Turkey. She was there preparing for an International Congress and was introduced to Kemal Ataturk, the country's dictator. She mentioned to him, in her quiet way, that it would be a splendid gift to give women the vote in the forthcoming election. Ataturk muttered something polite and non-committal, but a few months later Turkish women were given equal voting rights with men.

Despite her modern political outlook, she remained a true Victorian and in later life was shocked by the newfangled habit of calling people by their Christian names on short acquaintance – she wouldn't have dreamt of calling the vicar by his first name.

Dame Margery was never one to ignore a challenge. In her mid-90s, she was invited to view the newly restored Nutley windmill. As always when Dame Margery put in a public appearance, the press turned out in force. A photographer asked if she would pose pointing up at the sails.

"Well, if I do that I'm liable to fall over backwards," she answered, "but if I hold the secretary's arm, I shall be quite all right."

The secretary mentioned was from the Danehill Parish Historical Society. Still at Nutley, she was offered a chair to sit on while everyone went into the windmill, but she refused it forcefully. "What is the good of inviting me to come and see the windmill if I'm not going to be allowed to look over it?"

When it was explained that there were two vertical ladders to climb, she replied, "If you'll put somebody strong in front of me and somebody strong behind me in case I fall, I shall be quite all right." Without falling, she climbed to the very top.

At the age of 95, she made a second visit to Turkey to speak at celebrations commemorating Turkish women getting the vote. She travelled alone. Asked if her family worried about her going off on her own, she said, "Yes, my dear, they do, but if you can not do what you like when you are 95, you never will you know."

When she was 98, she admitted that the only gardening she could now do was weeding, which she did on her knees. She was very frail by then, but kept a whistle around her neck in case she fell and needed to attract her housekeeper's or handyman's attention.

"If I blow long, slow blasts," she explained, "they know that they can finish making the beds or washing the car before coming to help me up. But if I do short, agitated blasts, it means I've fallen into a patch of stinging-nettles and need immediate rescue.

Dame Margery died at the age of 99 and was buried at Horsted Keynes church on May 22nd 1981. On July 14th, a service of thanksgiving for her life and work was held at Westminster Abbey.

She was a much loved lady who has been greatly missed. She had a gift for instantly putting people at their ease and few women have done more to earn their place on the Honours List. On being congratulated on her D. B. B., she smiled and said with her gentle humour, "Well, it's nice to be given an honour so late in life that one isn't expected to do anything to deserve it." ❑

MARGARET FAIRLESS BARBER
(1869 – 1901)
MYSTIC WRITER

by Ann Feloy

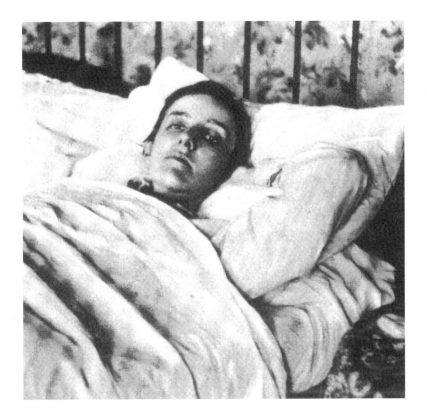

The tragic story of Margaret Fairless Barber has all but been forgotten. Yet in her day and for many decades after her untimely death at the age of 32, she earned the respect and affection of hundreds of thousands of women and men on both sides of the Atlantic.

Her book, The Roadmender, which was acclaimed as a classic, sold over 250,000 copies – a phenomenal amount even by today's standards. However, Margaret did not live long enough to enjoy the accolade she deserved. She was alive to see the chapters serialised in a national magazine, The Pilot, but her work was not published in book form until six months after her death in 1901.

It is therefore fitting that any book on notable Sussex women should include her as she wrote so poignantly about the Sussex countryside and its people.

Today, her book and other essays are to be found mainly in second-hand bookshops, yet she deserves to be remembered along with the more famous male literary figures, such as Hilaire Belloc, Tickner Edwardes and Richard Jefferies, whose work on Sussex lives on.

Born on May 7th 1869, Margaret Fairless Barber was the youngest of three children of a Yorkshire solicitor. Her elder sisters were called Agnes Marian and Mabel Alice. The three girls grew up in an educated and cultured environment: by the time she was 12 Margaret had read all the works of Scott and Dickens. After her formal education, she trained as a nurse and her first job was in a children's hospital attached to the Kilburn Sisterhood in Bermondsey.

Whilst nursing in the slums of London, she acquired the sobriquet 'the Fighting Sister' partly because she is supposed to have knocked a man down who was forcing his way into his sick wife's room and partly because she was not averse to stepping between antagonists who were fighting in the streets.

Margaret was a tireless worker and, as well as nursing during the day, she taught men's education classes in the evening. She was tall and very slim and her frail body often gave way under the constant demands she made on it because of her need to serve. In her childhood, she had contracted a spinal disease and this grew progressively worse – she would often have to go into hospital, as a patient, and remain there for months at a time. Her last nursing post was in Torquay, in her mid-20s, where she gained a reputation as a dedicated nurse, as well as a devoted Christian. After ill health forced her to give up nursing, she began to write, mainly for magazines.

Her parents had both died by the time she was 22 and she was financially independent. However, as she grew weaker, she had to be looked after constantly. She had a house in London on the Chelsea Embankment but preferred more and more to spend time in Sussex. "I am back in my own place, near the lean grey Downs, which keep watch and ward between the country and the sea," she wrote. It was at this time, according to her old school magazine, that she changed her name to Marjorie Dowson as she had adopted herself into the family of the 'medical lady' who had attended her in her frequent illnesses. At first she had rented a roadside country cottage, the lodge of Shermanbury Place, a house and estate deserted and run-down. She hired a very old woman as her maid and looked after a mentally retarded girl as her temporary ward.

The Times obituary of Margaret Fairless Barber recorded: "She gave food, patches and thread to tramps who marked her gateposts with safety signs against other tramps." In other words, she befriended those whom others shunned.

6

As she grew more frail, the Dowsons brought her to Mock Bridge House, near Henfield, very near the lodge she had rented. It may be wondered why Margaret was not looked after by one or other of her sisters. The eldest, Agnes, had married John Haggard and as her husband was in the consular service she was probably living abroad; the middle sister, Mabel, had married Joseph Oliver, a solicitor, but she was also in poor health and so not in a position to look after anyone else. Mabel, in fact, predeceased her younger sister.

Margaret possessed extraordinary strength of mind and, despite her affliction, was always determined to meet her magazine writing deadlines. When she was no longer able to sit, she lay with her notepad propped up on her chest so that she could write. As she weakened she lost the use of her right hand so she learned to write with her left. For days on end she was unable to take solid food.

Although known as Majorie all her life, Margaret used the pseudonym 'Michael Fairless' for her writing. It was derived from a childhood friend, Michael McDonald (later he was knighted and became the Chief Justice of Palestine) and her middle name which was a family name on her father's side. Only a handful of people knew her true identity. Her increasingly devoted readership in The Pilot magazine did not know they were reading the work of a woman, nor did they know of her acute suffering.

Margaret spent the last years of her life growing ever more paralysed and increasingly bedridden. *The Roadmender* was written at Mock Bridge House in the last 20 months of her life. She died, almost completely blind, fighting for every last breath to dictate the final words of her book:

"But beyond the white gate and the trail of woodbine falls the silence greater than speech, darkness greater than light, a pause, of a little while, and then the touch of that healing garment as we pass to the King in His beauty, in a land from which there is no return. At the gateway I cry you farewell."

The public was unaware, too, of the exact location of the book for although she wrote vividly of "the little church at the foot of the grey-green Down . . . the white gate . . . the field of daffodils", no church, hill, village or lane was ever named. All of this helped to explain why Margaret Fairless Barber, the person, remained as much a mystery as her book for almost 20 years after her death.

Slowly, however, following her death, the details of 'Michael Fairless' began to emerge. People were stunned to find that the writer was a woman and a former nurse. But no more details of her life came to light until 12 years after she died when a small volume titled *Michael Fairless, Life and Writings* was published jointly by her sister Agnes and closest friend, Mrs Dowson, the 'medical lady' who had nursed her right up until the end. Even these minimal details were only grudgingly given on the grounds that if authorised information was not forthcoming, something unauthorised and incorrect would be issued. To the frustration of the literary critics and the reading public alike, even then it was not divulged that Sussex was the location of the book.

It was not until 1921 that an article by Arthur Henry Anderson was published in *The Observer* claiming the successful identification of the scenes of *The Roadmender*, to commemorate the 20th anniversary of the writer's death. Such was the fascination and interest created that Anderson followed the article with a book, in 1924, entitled *The Roadmender's Country*.

In it, Anderson described how he had made a detailed study of the work and the memorial volume, and an incidental reference had led him to believe the county described might be Sussex. "I settled down to a careful study of the Ordnance Map," he wrote, "with a view to finding what part of the county might answer all the requirements: where might be found not only the winding white road, the monastery bell, the lean grey Downs, the reeded waters of the sequestered pool."

He found the first clue to the location of *The Roadmender* in the churchyard at Shermanbury. The book mentions some fir trees and the writer makes a request: that he/she be buried under them. Shermanbury churchyard had some firs, trees which were not at all common to that part of Sussex, but Anderson could find no grave there. He continued to search in other graveyards nearby.

Along the River Adur from Shermanbury, Anderson went into the 12th century parish church of St James at Ashurst. In the churchyard he found a simple wooden cross, some five feet high, inscribed with the words: "Lo, How I Loved Thee" and the name Margaret Fairless Dowson . . .

In *The Roadmender,* the author narrates scenes of rural life, through the eyes of a man who earns his living breaking up stones by the roadside to mend the highways – a common occupation at the turn of the century. She writes: "All gifts are mine as I sit by the winding white road and serve the footsteps of my fellows."

The road she describes is the north and south road from Beeding and Henfield to Cowfold and Horsham or East Grinstead. And forever immortalised in the book is the delightful area of Downland and Weald embracing Poynings, Edburton, Fulking, Wiston, Steyning and Shoreham.

In reality, she could see across the garden to "the stretch of grassland and the winding road beyond, with hedge and tangle of traveller's joy, woodbine, sweet briar and late roses" and the mystical "white gate" – all from her own room as she lay bedridden,

"This garden is an epitome of peace; the sun, rain, flowers and birds gather me into the blessedness of their active harmony," she wrote. Her description of the view from her own window and the sound of the monastery bell at St Hugh. near Cowfold, were another two of the clues that eventually led to the detection of the writer's last home.

Another passage, it was later revealed, was inspired by the Adur valley, among the Downs above Shoreham where Margaret had once stood on the summit "hatless, the smack of salt on my cheek, all around me rolling stretches of cloud-shadowed Down, no sound but the shrill mourn of the peewit and the gathering of the sea.

In the book *The Roadmender* recalls the wayfarers he meets: the tramps, the four-year-old child whose mother died 'in childbed' and the grandmother 'tall, angular, dauntless, good for another ten years of hard work.' He recalls the funeral cart and the droves of sheep and cattle on route to the 'fair at B.', as well as the impoverished old couple who part along the road, with him going on alone to the Workhouse.

The Roadmender hammers out his thoughts on life and death and the vast changes happening in the year Queen Victoria died. There is an overwhelming serenity about the work and *The Times* recorded: "The fresh beauty and mystical tone of the book appealed to workmen and queens alike."

For more than three decades the writings of Margaret Fairless Barber enjoyed enormous popularity. A visit to her grave became a pilgrimage for large numbers of people from this country and abroad. It is ironic in the light of her present virtual anonymity that a foreword to one of her numerous editions should state: "Certainly no book of our time is so clearly marked for the crown of immortality . . ."

The First World War had brought despair and suffering to Britain and *The Roadmender* helped to heal the ravages and scars left on a grieving nation. The words touched a chord in the hearts of many, ringing out in the quiet of their souls.

It is unclear why Margaret preferred to use a pseudonym rather than the name she was born with or even the name she adopted. It is known that she hated publicity and believed her mission in life was to serve humanity rather than reap any personal glory. Furthermore, she believed herself and the book's location to be unimportant. These details were irrelevant, in her mind perhaps, to the spiritual, homespun philosophy she embraced in her short life and which she wished to share – a homespun yet eternal philosophy which is captured in the opening of *The Roadmender.*

"What do we ask of life, here or indeed hereafter, but leave to serve, to live, to commune with our fellow men and with ourselves . . .". ❏

LADY ANNE BLUNT
(1837-1917)

JUDITH BLUNT, LADY WENTWORTH
(1873-1957)

THE ARABIAN HORSE – SUCH PERFECT BEAUTY FROM THE BARREN WASTES

T here are few animals more beautiful than the Arab horse. With their gazelle-like heads, arched necks and flowing manes, they are now a familiar sight at horse shows everywhere. They parade around the ring with a light, dancing stride, ears pricked, tails high, looking as if they have never been anything other than the stars of the horse world. And yet, without the efforts of Lady Anne Blunt, her husband and her daughter, Judith, the breed might have been lost forever.

Lady Anne was the grand-daughter of Lord Byron and daughter of the first Earl of Lovelace. She was an extremely attractive woman, well-educated in comparison with many women born in the mid- 19th century, and a talented artist and violinist – she was also surprisingly diffident and described herself as "the most commonplace of mortals". She was already in her thirties in 1869 when she married Wilfrid Scawen Blunt the poet, publicist and political activist. Wilfrid had been a British diplomat before turning against the British Establishment and its imperialist policy. He championed the cause of Arab, Egyptian and Irish freedom and later in life was imprisoned for his part in the struggle for Home Rule in Ireland.

It was Wilfrids ill-health which led him and his wife to discover the beauty of the Arab horses. Wilfrid's mother, sister and brother had all died of TB and he had also contracted the disease. The damp British climate was aggravating his condition and, on medical advice, he and Lady Anne began travelling abroad. They went to countries with hot, dry climates – Spain. Algeria, Turkey, Iraq, Egypt – and in order to make the most of the air, they travelled mainly on horseback.

Anne was the first European woman to penetrate the heart of Arabia where her remarkable physical endurance won the respect of the local tribesmen and their leaders. She was a distinguished Arabic scholar. Having learnt the language from a Sheikh in Cairo, she spoke it fluently and was even known to use it when responding to the Catholic Mass. Both she and her husband were fascinated by the desert horses. Wilfrid wrote:

"It seemed nothing less than a miracle to find in those deserted and barren wastes a thing of such perfect beauty." But the beauty was under threat. The Bedouin thought of their horses as the soil and had always said, "We cannot sell the earth." But times were changing and many could no longer afford to keep their best breeding stock. City and town dwelling Arabs frequently ill-treated their horses and most were cross-bred with inferior strains.

When his brother had died in 1872, Wilfrid had inherited the estates of Crabbet Park and Newbuildings Place and he and Anne had designed and built a 17th century style house at Crabbet near Crawley. An entry in Anne's journal written in Syria in 1877 said: "We have made a plan of importing some of the best Arazeh blood to England and breeding it pure there. It would be an interesting and useful thing to do."

Together, she and Wilfrid visited all the great horse-breeding tribes of the northern deserts of Arabia, seeking out the last genuine breeders and buying their best stallions and mares. The horses were shipped home and installed at Crabbet and Newbuildings and the Crabbet Arabian Stud was founded in 1878. The following year, Anne and Wilfrid travelled to Nejd, the territory of the Emir of Ha'il, and increased their numbers to 25 brood mares and stallions. Generation by generation, the horses improved under the selective breeding pattern imposed by Lady Anne and her husband and, in 1896, the line was refined even further by six mares and four stallions saved from the once celebrated stud of the Viceroy of Egypt, Ali Pasha Sherif By the time the Crabbet Arabian Stud was founded, Anne and Wilfrid's daughter, Judith, was about five years old and it was already obvious that she had inherited her parents' love of horses. Throughout her life she continued their work, improving the Arabs further so that they grew larger, looked even more beautiful and became better riding horses. She revolutionised their feeding regime and carried out some original research which led to an understanding of the uniqueness of the Arab's skeleton. She had her grooms dissect any foals that died and found they had one less vertebra than other breeds giving them a greater capacity for carrying weight and endurance.

Anne, Wilfrid and Judith had a rare gift which allowed them to sense the possibilities in each horse and combination of horses and to create the conditions which would fulfil their potential. Unfortunately, they weren't so adept at producing successful human relationships. Wilfrid generated scandal. He was as devoted to his daughter as Judith was to him, but she found it increasingly difficult to accept his unfaithfulness to her mother. When she was in her early twenties, she discovered he had made a young married friend of hers pregnant and some time later, he looked as if he might do the same to another of her friends – until she put a stop to it. It was the beginning of a family feud which lasted on and off all their lives.

In 1906, Anne and Wilfrid separated and the horses were split between them. Anne spent her summers at Crabbet and her winters in Egypt. A prolific writer, she had several books published including *Journey to Nejd* and Bedouins of the Euphrates. While she was in Egypt in 1916, she was cut off by the U-boat campaign. She died the following year not long after she had succeeded to the barony of Wentworth. Judith was as attractive as her mother had been and could be very charming – she could also be extremely perverse, rarely trusting anyone, including her own family. In 1899, she had married the Hon. Neville Bulwer-Lytton and as a marriage settlement Wilfrid had given her Crabbet Park. The marriage produced a son and two daughters, but eventually ended in divorce.

When her mother died in 1917, Judith inherited the title of Lady Wentworth, but Lady Anne's share of the stud was supposed to go to her grand-daughters. Wilfrid felt the horses should come to him, and he and Judith entered into a legal battle which lasted three years. When the case was finally being decided, the court had to assemble at Newbuildings. Wilfrid, by then old and ill, wore Arab dress as he lay on his bed surrounded by the judge and court officials. He lost the case and when he died about two years later, his body was wrapped in a travelling rug and buried without ceremony in the Newbuildings woods.

Although Judith had fought for her children's right to the horses, as she grew older, she became more and more jealous and often alienated them. After the Second World War, she led strong local opposition towards the plan to enlarge the village of Crawley into a new town. She spoke her mind at a public inquiry held in the village hall opposite Three Bridges railway station in November 1946 and the meeting ended in uproar. Like her mother, Judith was a prolific author and wrote many books. *The Arabian Horse and His Descendants*, published in 1945, was one of her major works. She was a fine sculptor and also a proficient sportswoman. For most of her life she played billiards, squash and real tennis, the precursor of modern lawn tennis. Eccentric to the end, she gave herself the title of 'world's lady tennis champion' – an accolade which was repeated under her entry in Who Was Who despite the fact that she had never played a single match against another woman.

Judith died in 1957 when she was 84. As a passing shot at her family, she left her horses not to her daughters, but to her estate manager. However, in spite of her tempestuous character, she had consolidated the work her parents had begun. Most of the Arab horses in this country   today are descended from Crabbet stock, as are many in Russia, America and other parts of the world. In recent years, there has been a revival of interest within the Arab nations in their native horses and Crabbet Arabians have now moved full circle and have been exported back to Arabia where Lady Anne first found them. ❏

BARBARA BODICHON
(1827- 1891)

LANDSCAPE PAINTER, TIRELESS CAMPAIGNER

B arbara Bodichon was that interesting kind of woman who could be both famous and prosaic. She became an accomplished and successful artist in her own lifetime and still managed to keep her feet firmly on the ground. Barbara was born in a village near Battle on April 8th 1827, into a family which was both practical and radical. Her grandfather was one of the Liberal MIPs who fought against slavery and her father, Benjamin Leigh-Smith, was a wealthy landowner who became the MIP for Norwich. Florence Nightingale, who needs no introduction other than her name, was Barbara's first cousin.

When his wife died young, Benjamin could easily have sent Barbara away to live with relatives or made other arrangements for her upbringing – common practice in those days – but he was a devoted father and preferred to keep his children close by his side. He enrolled them at Westminster Infant's School – a pioneering establishment run by the eccentric, James Buchanan, a follower of Emanuel Swedenborg, the religious teacher who claimed to be in direct contact with the spiritual world. At home, Barbara spent many hours with her father and his political friends. He did all he could to help develop both her intellect and her artistic nature, and at the same time encouraged her to take up social and charitable works. When she was 21, he made her an allowance of £300, because he saw no reason why girls shouldn't have the same financial independence that boys were given automatically. Many would have considered his gift a bizarre indulgence.

Barbara's artistic talent was progressing and she decided to concentrate her energies towards improving her technique. In 1849, she enrolled at Bedford College, a university college for women which had recently been opened in London, and she began laying the foundations which would one day help her to become a celebrated landscape painter. Having been intellectually stimulated from an early age herself, she was naturally interested in education and she spent some time studying primary education in London. The result of her research was Portman Hall School which she opened in 1852 in Paddington. Understandably, when you think of her own schooling, Portman Hall was an unconventional mixed establishment that catered for children of all creeds and social classes. Many of the teachers were volunteers and their work was frequently experimental. Apart from the usual subjects, they taught elementary physiology, social economy and science. Although the weekly cost of the education was 18 pence per pupil, Barbara only charged the working class children sixpence, making up the difference herself She ran the school for ten years with the help of her friend, Elizabeth Whitehead.

During her late 20s, she became increasingly concerned with the predicament of unhappily married women and their lack of property rights. Mobilising her friends, she began a petition which was signed by 3,000 women, many of them notable figures in the arts and sciences like Harriet Martineau and Elizabeth Barrett Browning. The petition was presented to the House of Lords by Lord Brougham and to the House of Commons by Sir Erskine Parry. Success wasn't immediate, but the resulting Married Women's Property Bill eventually changed the laws governing marriage and divorce. In 1857, the year she married Dr Eugene Bodichon, a French physician who lived in Algiers, she wrote *Women and Work.*

The Bodichons spent a year after their marriage visiting cities in America and Canada where Barbara put her artistic talent to good use and painted what became some of her most popular works. Her *Falls of Niagara* was received with critical acclaim and exhibitions of her work were held in Philadelphia and Washington as well as in London. Her pictures were so popular that they sold almost before they were dry.

While she was abroad, she kept detailed diaries of her travels which were later featured in magazines. She continued her painting on a subsequent trip to Brittany and the water-colours were exhibited at the French Gallery in Pall Mall.

In 1858, she helped finance *The English Woman's Journal*, a magazine concerned mainly with the educational and industrial interests of women. She read the first paper on suffrage and having supported the first suffrage petition, she became Secretary of the Suffrage Committee in 1867.

She spent her winters in Algiers in the villa on the hills above the city, overlooking the sea and the plain. The Bodichons entertained a great deal and Barbara became involved with the Orphelinat, a local institute for orphans. She also began planting trees, Eucalyptus trees, which had been found to improve conditions in areas infested with malaria – the fragrant oil from the leaves discouraging mosquitoes and the roots absorbing excess water from the soil.

The summers in England were spent working to improve the situation of women. She was particularly interested in the right of women to higher education. Financially, as well as physically, she helped Emily Davies found a college at Hitchin in 1869. Three years later, it moved to Cambridge and became Girton College.

Throughout her years of campaigning for feminist rights, she continued her painting – her *Cornfield after a Storm* attracted Ruskin's attention and her pictures were exhibited at the Royal Academy. They continued to sell successfully, although Barbara never painted for financial gain and much of the money received for her work went towards helping students and creating scholarships.

She never tired of travel and everywhere she went her brushes and palette were put to work. She painted cedar forests in the Atlas Mountains, Arabs fishing, black women making a sacrifice in Algiers, the Alhambra as it rises out of Granada. But much of her most emotive work was produced in Sussex. She painted scenes of Hastings in the early morning, of Beachy Head with the waves crashing on the chalk beach, of bad weather in St. Leonards.

She was still painting and campaigning when she died in 1891. French critics had called her the Rosa Bonheur of landscape, but perhaps the greatest accolade came from the writer, George Eliot. In her youth, Barbara had been very beautiful and her vitality and determination made her the inspiration for Eliot's *Romola*. ❏

CORNELIA CONNELLY
(1809-1879)
THE NEXT SUSSEX SAINT?

The life of Cornelia Connelly could almost be the stuff of fiction. Her story is one of amazing courage, self-sacrifice and devotion. She was born Comelia Augusta Peacock in Philadelphia on January 15th 1809. Her family was highly respectable and she grew into a beautiful, well-educated young woman.

As she reached maturity, she came under the influence of a charismatic young Episcopalian minister called Pierce Connelly and in 1831 they married. Cornelia was 22 years old and deeply in love. The couple made their first home in Natchez, Mississippi, where Pierce continued his ministry as Rector of Holy Trinity Church. Their first two children, Mercer and Adeline, were born there.

During their time at Natchez, the Connellys began investigating allegations against the Catholic Church. Having met and been strongly influenced by a number of Catholics, Pierce decided to resign his Episcopalian ministry and to confirm his new faith by going to Rome. Cornelia herself was already convinced of the truth of Catholicism and with her two children was received into the Catholic church in New Orleans. The whole family then set sail for Europe. In Rome they were granted an interview with the Pope and shortly afterwards, Pierce was also received into the church.

The next two years were spent mainly in Rome under the patronage of Lord Shrewsbury, a fervent Catholic, and the Borghese family. Cornelia became friends with Gwendaline, Lord Shrewsbury's daughter and wife of the heir to the Borghese fortune. Gwendaline's piety had gained her the title of the 'Angel of Rome' and her charitable works were not lost on Cornelia. When Lord Shrewsbury invited Pierce to his home in Staffordshire, Cornelia stayed behind with her children and forged closer links with Rome. Her husband spent the summer enjoying the hospitality of a succession of stately homes in England. It was 1836.

When Pierce returned, Cornelia became pregnant again and after John Henry was born, they all returned to America and to Grand Coteau, Louisiana. Home became a cottage in the grounds of the Jesuit school where Pierce was teaching and for 18 months life was idyllic. Cornelia worked too, teaching music at the Sacred Heart Convent school nearby and rekindling her interest in education.

It was then that the first tragedy struck. In July 1839, Cornelia gave birth to a little girl who died when she was just two months old. The loss affected Cornelia deeply, but if anything, it strengthened her faith and she confessed later that her years at Grand Coteau were the happiest of her life. One day in January 1840, she stood in her garden. Overwhelmed by joy, she prayed, "My God, if all this happiness is not to thy greater glory and the good of souls take it from me – I make the sacrifice."

It seems a strange request, but perhaps she sensed her husband's growing dissatisfaction with his life and foresaw the consequences.

Then came a second, even greater tragedy.

Cornelia's youngest son, John Henry, was two-and-a-half years old and full of bright mischief like most children of that age. He managed to escape his nurse and run into the garden to play with the Connellys' Newfoundland. As the boy and dog romped together, they came too close to a sugar-boiler which had been left to cool by the back door. The dog leapt and John Henry was thrown into the scalding liquid.

For two days and nights, Cornelia held the tortured body of her child in her arms. Nothing could be done to save him.

Over the previous months, Cornelia had been practising a prayer of resignation and she needed it now. Nine months later, when she was pregnant with her fifth child, she needed it again. Walking back from Mass one day, Pierce told Cornelia he wanted to return to the priesthood. In order to take up the celibate life of a Catholic priest, he explained that she would probably be required to enter a convent.

The test had come. She loved her husband and her children, but she also loved her God and less than a year earlier she had offered to give up her happiness if He should ask that sacrifice of her. Cornelia agreed. Nothing was done in a rush. She gave birth to another baby boy who was christened Frank and in 1842, Pierce took Mercer to school in England on his way to put his case before the Vatican. Cornelia moved to a small house by the convent at Grand Coteau and began preparing herself for a cloistered life. Eventually, the summons came from Rome and once there she gave the formal consent that would allow Pierce to follow his vocation and signed a deed of separation.

At her own request, she went to stay with the Sacred Heart nuns and lived the life of a postulant in a cottage in the convent grounds with her youngest son and his nurse.

Her daughter, Adeline, became a boarder at the school there. After Pierce had spent a year training and before he could become a full-fledged priest, Cornelia was asked to take a vow of chastity. She gave her husband one last chance to return to their married life, an offer which Pierce declined. Having secured a promise from the Cardinal Vicar that she wouldn't necessarily have to enter a religious order and would still be able to care for her children, she took the solemn vow and on July 6th 1845, Pierce was ordained.

The years that followed were not happy ones. It was quite obvious Cornelia wasn't suited to the isolated life and the church authorities only asked her to follow a relaxed regime in comparison to the Sisters. She was allowed to see Pierce periodically and together they mapped out a future for her which involved starting an apostolic community. Apart from Mercer, who was still being educated in England, the children were with her and although she expected them to stay for several more years, she felt the call from God growing ever stronger. Asked to formalise her ideas for the community, she wrote: "The congregation is wholly for the works of spiritual mercy. The sisters are not cloistered and the dress is the least striking possible."

She wanted the community to be called a society, not to be confused with a monastic order and intended the focus to be Jesus – the name that came to her was the 'Society of the Holy Child Jesus' . Although, her wish was to return to America, the Pope thought otherwise and she was sent to England to take charge of a large poor school and convent in Derby. A near stranger to this country and with little money and few friends, it was a great challenge, but Cornelia arrived in Derby and founded her Society.

By the end of 1846, all seemed well. She had begun her year's training as a novice and been joined by other converts. But then Pierce arrived. He had come to England as assistant chaplain at Lord Shrewsbury's home and he wanted to continue seeing Cornelia and take a hand in running the Society. Access was forbidden, but he took no notice, and Cornelia, who considered her vows sacrosanct, was forced to ask him to leave her and the Society alone. He reacted by snatching the children from their schools and taking them abroad.

He went to Rome and returned later saying he had papal authority to see his wife, but she refused to see him until he had at least brought Adeline back. Again she told him he was to have nothing more to do with the Society or its regulations. An eyewitness said Pierce threw himself on a sofa and remained there for six hours in a passion of rage and disappointment when he heard Cornelia's ultimatum. He abandoned his priesthood and said he would, "rescue his wife from the hands of devils."

Now we come to Sussex, or rather Cornelia came. The community in Derby developed financial problems and it was suggested she move to a property in St. Leonards-on-Sea and develop a centre for Catholics scattered along thirty miles of the Sussex coast. She had only been in residence for six weeks when she was served with a writ. Pierce was suing for restoration of his conjugal rights.

Having once put her aside with such determination, his about-turn was equally determined, not to say barefaced. He wrote at the time:

'I am a man, a husband and a father before I am a priest and my first duties cannot be abandoned ... I will now never cease until Mrs. Connelly is placed absolutely and unreservedly under my control.'

In a time when women were considered subject to men in almost every respect, it's perhaps not surprising that when the case came before the Court of Arches in May, 1849, judgement was given in Pierce's favour. Cornelia's council appealed. The case had caught the imagination of the public and *The Times* published daily reports of the proceedings. Cornelia was hounded and threatened, forced to keep a disguise in her cell and never allowed out alone. In 1851, the judgement against her was reversed and the case referred for retrial, but, by this time, the court costs had left Pierce penniless. In an act of charity, Cornelia paid the debts herself to save him from prison.

The case was finally closed in 1856 and by then Cornelia had received another blow with the news that her eldest son, Mercer, had died in New

Orleans unreconciled to the Catholic faith. Pierce, true to his word, never ceased his campaign and over the next 20 years wrote a series of letters and pamphlets attacking the Catholic church, continually causing problems for Cornelia and her community. He returned eventually to the Episcopalian church and lived with Adeline in Florence until his death in 1883.

Who knows what effect such years of torment had on Cornelia? She never allowed her feelings to show in public, continuing her labours with dignity and tranquillity. Her Society grew and strengthened as she worked tirelessly in the cause of education and the relief of suffering. She trained sisters to teach and sent them to schools in London, Preston and Blackpool. The college at St. Leonards continued to thrive and an early inspector's report said: 'It is impossible to witness without admiration the results obtained in this very interesting school in which consummate skill in the art of teaching, unwearied patience and the most persuasive personal influence have combined to accomplish all the rarest fruits of Christian instruction. The school is now probably one of the most perfect institutions of its class in Europe.'

In the early 1860s, the Dowager Duchess of Leeds gave the Society the site of the old episcopal palace at Mayfield to build a convent and school. The palace itself was in total ruin and had become a favourite picnicking spot for Victorian society. Anyone else would have pulled down the remaining walls and started again. Cornelia rebuilt them, restoring the palace to its former glory and founding an educational society which still flourishes today.

To her great sorrow, and mainly due to Pierce, Rome refused to approve the regulations that formed the rules for the Society during her lifetime. She did see her daughter once or twice more and reconciled Adeline to the Catholic faith. Her remaining son, Frank, became a well-known sculptor. He was never fully reconciled to the church, but sent his daughter, Marina, to school at the last convent Cornelia founded at Neuilly in France.

Is it possible she found rest and peace in Sussex? Probably not. In later life, she admitted privately to a friend that the Society of the Holy Child Jesus was founded on a broken heart.

On April 18th 1879, after many months of painful illness, Cornelia died. It was 33 years to the day since she had left Rome on her Holy mission. At her own request, she was buried in the little convent cemetery at Mayfield. In 1935, Cornelia's body was exhumed in order to be transferred to a memorial tomb within the convent chapel. Although 56 years had passed since her death, she was still completely recognisable.

The long journey towards sainthood goes on. Her work continues in many parts of the world and her province in West Africa is thriving. On June 13th 1992, Cornelia was formally recognised as a woman of The inscription on Cornelia's tomb in the chapel at Mayfield reads:

'Love knoweth no measure,
feareth no labour,
Maketh sweet all that is bitter,
Findeth rest in God alone.' ❏

MARIE CORBETT
(1859-1932)
500 GRATEFUL BABIES

Marie Corbett's driving force was the fierce sense of obligation she felt towards those less fortunate than herself, particularly children. During her lifetime, 500 babies passed through her hands and every one of them had cause to thank her.

Marie was born in 1859 when the Victorian era was firmly established. She was the daughter of George and Eliza Gray of Tunbridge Wells. Her father was a gifted entrepreneur who made his fortune in confectionery and preserves. Both he and his wife were liberal and extremely progressive.

Although it was unfashionable at the time, Marie and her sister, Cicely, were given a comprehensive education which equalled that of their brother, Adrian. As she grew up, Marie developed into an exceptionally strong and determined character. In 1881, she married a barrister named Charles Corbett. In some ways they were an unlikely couple. Marie was much taller than her husband and they were very different in temperament.

They were, however, devoted to each other. Each shared the other's progressive outlook and this made for a very happy marriage.

They made their home at Woodgate, a large, formidable-looking house in Danehill. Luxuries were of no interest to either of them, although they could easily afford comfort. The lack of central heating and inelegant furnishings eventually became a joke among their many friends, but the Corbetts were interested in people not possessions. Tenants and locals from miles around frequently tramped to Woodgate for advice – Charles would help with legal problems, while personal matters were always taken to Marie. At a time when the wealthy regularly turned out servant girls who became pregnant, the Corbetts took on a young housemaid who had been in trouble repeatedly. She became pregnant again while she was with them, but they kept her on.

Knowing the locals had no means of transport, if Marie was driving to town in her pony and trap, she would send a message down to the village asking if anyone needed a lift to the hospital or the workhouse, or to visit friends. She cut an unusual figure among the prim and proper of Victorian society. Although she didn't actually ride, she was often seen striding around the village or town dressed in a pair of riding breeches of her own design. She would wear them to garden parties too, acknowledging the occasion by simply adding a hat.

In the 1906 Liberal landslide, Charles fought for and won the parliamentary seat of East Grinstead. It had been considered a safe Conservative seat and the result was a sensation. Marie had campaigned for him tirelessly, but she was never destined to be simply the good woman behind a great man. By then, she was already a political force in her own right.

Marie Corbett was one of the first women in the country to be elected as a Poor Law Guardian and became the first woman on Uckfield Rural District Council. Through her position on the Uckfield Board of Guardians for the workhouse, she was to spend 36 years working on behalf of friendless children. A mother herself by then, Marie was horrified by the fact that the local workhouse carefully separated husbands and wives, but mixed the children in with the old women, some of whom were mentally handicapped. Determined to do something, she set about finding people in the community who were willing to open their homes and gradually she began emptying the workhouse of children. Every child was visited regularly and the foster parents were paid for their keep. Marie's grandson, Dr Michael Ashby, remembers her coming down to breakfast at Woodgate on one of her visiting days carrying a half inch thick wad of crisp ten shilling notes which made his eyes bulge.

She had no patience with officialdom if it hindered the children's welfare. A government inspector checking the foster homes for suitability said she didn't approve of one woman because her cottage was too untidy. Marie answered, "If she smacks the child when it's naughty and kisses it when it's good, it won't matter about anything else."

At one time, she had 40 children to visit every month and 100 under her care. When she had succeeded in emptying the Uckfield workhouse, she turned her attention to one at Eastbourne and one in London. Marie was half way through rescuing the children from the Brighton workhouse when she died in 1932. She was 73 years old.

As part of her obituary, The *Mid-Sussex Times* said, 'Danehill in particular and the country in general are poorer through the death of Mrs Marie Corbett . . . No one could be near her without realising how rare and beautiful her character.'

In the weeks that followed, her family received letters from all over the world. They came from children, now grown into adults, who said their whole lives had been transformed by the loving start they had been given with the families Marie had found for them.

Her passing was an immense loss, but she left a wealth of happy memories to those who had known her and she left all of us a legacy of great value, another of our Sussex Women, her daughter, Dame Margery Corbett Ashby. ❏

MILLY DAYRELL
(1879-1969)

ECCENTRIC CHICKEN BREEDER

She was christened Violet Elizabeth Mildred Dayrell, but was always known as Milly. She was a product of two generations of clergymen. Her grandfather had been a parson and her father was the Reverend Francis R. Dayrell of Aberystwyth. Francis Dayrell was an intimidating man who rather enjoyed striking fear into a congregation and he wasn't above doing the same for his family. Possibly as a reaction to his father, Milly's brother Frank, who was three years younger than she was, became a wastrel and a philanderer – he spent his life racing fast cars and disposing of what there was of the family fortune. Milly's reaction was to become a strong, self-reliant woman. She never married.

Milly was born on Christmas Day. 1879, and named after her mother, Violet. Like most girls of her class, she was educated at home by a governess while her brother was sent away to school. It was already becoming obvious that Frank had a weak character and Milly compensated by taking on family responsibilities which should have fallen to him as the only son. She escaped as soon as she could and came to live in Sussex at Marigolds Farm in the parish of Hellingly and started keeping chickens and a few cows, selling the milk and eggs at Lewes and Hailsham markets.

Put like that, her life at Marigolds sounds very tame.

But Milly was only interested in being the best – whatever she laid her hands on had to be a success.

She started collecting different types of chicken, specialising in Speckled Sussex, Light Sussex, White Leghorns and Buff Orpingtons – and she applied her highly developed practical streak to their breeding programme. At the Great National Poultry, Pigeon and Rabbit Show at Crystal Palace in 1905, she was awarded a Bronze Medal for her invention, 'The Hen'. The brochure read: 'Miss Dayrell, Marigolds farm, Hellingly, Sussex, showed a new brooder known as the Hen Combination Foster Mother. This is on distinctly original lines. The brooder is divided up into departments, each to contain fifteen chickens, and in each division there is a stuffed hen heated by hot water. The chicks nestle under the hen's feathers. The hens can be removed and the foster mother turned into a cold brooder.' – Farm and Garden, November 18th, 1905.

When Milly's father died, she moved the short distance to The Hale at Hale Green, near Chiddingly, and her mother came down from Wales and went to live with their great friend, Grace Reeves, nearby.

At Hale, Milly began farming on a larger scale, increasing her livestock breeding activities to include cows and collecting more and more chicken - friends often gave her unusual breeds as birthday presents. She was the absolute ruler on the farm. At hay-making time, she would build and thatch the haystacks herself with the skill of a professional thatcher.

During the First World War, she took on the task of training Land Girls and she probably led them quite a dance. She couldn't abide cowards. No one was ever allowed to avoid doing anything she wanted them to do.

She was sitting in the house one day when she saw a blue flash go up from the middle of her cornfields. She informed the military and they apprehended a German spy. It turned out he had been using the fields as a signalling position. Milly, always ready to add drama to her stories, later described him as a terrifying creature dressed all in black, his head covered by a black hood.

In a different life, Milly could have been an adventurer. Holidays were often taken with her friend, The Lady Julian Parr. They travelled to places like the Pyrenees, crossing the mountains on foot with donkeys and traversing gorges by means of precarious rope bridges. Even for holidays closer to home, she preferred the unusual and designed and built her own horse-drawn covered-wagon – an English version of those used to tame the Wild West.

In the Second World War, she was an ARP Warden and had a rifle range on her land. She also had the misfortune to have billeted on her three London County Council schoolmasters who seemed to think everyone at Hale was some sort of servant.

Her talent for organisation wasn't restricted to the farm. In Chiddingly, she founded the Horticultural Society and the Women's Institute and she was elected first Secretary, then President of the WI. County Federation. She was a Church Warden, a School Inspector, a Governor of Hellingly Hospital, a Hailsham and District Councillor and the local Stoolball Captain. She was also a Fellow of the Royal Photographic Society and she had some of her work exhibited – which she had processed in her own dark-room at Hale. She took photographs of everything around the farm and village and many of her pictures were of professional standard, although they weren't necessarily for sale. Milly took photos for the 'sheer excitement' not for money, but she liked people to see them, just as she liked to exhibit everything else she produced.

In her 40s, she was preparing a bull she had bred for the show ring and was leading it around a field by the regulation stick and chain attached to the ring in its nose. She slipped and the startled bull charged off around the field. Milly, being Milly, wouldn't let go of the stick and the result was two broken legs and a damaged knee that gave her trouble for the rest of her life – it didn't stop her showing livestock, though.

When she was in her 60s, something similar happened.

The bees in one of the hives she kept swarmed and she was stung over 100 times. Her whole body came up like a balloon – but again, it didn't stop her keeping bees. She was very protective of all her animals. A fox killed several of her prize chickens one night and at four the next morning, Milly was up a tree with her shotgun. The only thing anyone saw of the fox after that was its brush which Milly had mounted and hung in her hall. She was 74 years old at the time.

Milly was 89 when she died in 1969. Her final years were lived in austere conditions with no heating and little money – family and friends provided her meals. She had spent her last 15 years alone at Hale, guarded by her six cats and a revolver which she fired out of the window if she heard a noise. ❏

CHRISTIANA EDMUNDS
(1827-1905)
THE CHOCOLATE CREAM MURDERER

With the constant diet of police and crime drama fed to us by the media these days, you could be forgiven for reading the account of Christiana Edmunds and thinking you were running through the script of the latest Sunday night who-done-it. The story line has all the right ingredients, obsession and love, murder and madness.

Christiana was born in Margate in 1827, the daughter of a respected architect and his wife. Her father died when he was in his mid-40s and she and her remaining family moved to Brighton to live in Gloucester Place. By the time she was 42, both her brother and her sister had also met with untimely deaths and Christiana and her mother were living alone.

After the fashion of the day, the two women took a stroll along the promenade whenever the weather permitted and one particular day, a man glanced at Christiana as he was walking by. It was a natural thing to do - she was an elegant woman who looked younger than her years, tall and of fair complexion. Christiana returned the glance . . . and fell in love.

Over the next few days, she made a point of discovering the man's identity. She learnt he was a local doctor by the name of Beard and found out where he lived. She also learned he had a wife and children, but Christiana discounted them. She was already becoming obsessed.

Pretending to be ill, she told her mother she had heard of an excellent doctor and asked her to arrange for him to attend her in Gloucester Place. Her mother did as she was requested and Dr Beard duly visited his new patient.

There was no denying Christiana was an attractive woman and presumably the doctor was flattered by the interest she made no attempt to hide. If he didn't encourage her, he certainly put little effort towards discouraging her and their friendship developed quickly. He secretly kept the letters she began sending, long letters, written in a way that would have been impossible to misinterpret. He took her to his home and introduced her to his family and Christiana soon became a regular visitor, making herself agreeable to his wife, if only while they were in the same room.

Until this point in the story nothing untoward had happened. Dr Beard had behaved foolishly in keeping Christiana's letters and possibly under-estimating her feelings for him, but in his defence, she probably wasn't the first female patient to develop a crush on her physician. Now the story took a more sinister turn.

One day, Christiana arrived at the Beard house while the doctor was out. His wife greeted her and invited her into the drawing-room where they sat talking together for some time. During the conversation, Christiana produced a box of chocolate creams which she said were of a particularly fine flavour. In a light-hearted way, she popped one into Mrs Beard's mouth and her hostess had swallowed part of the sweet before realising it actually tasted horrible and spitting it out. Christiana was contrite and quickly offered her another sweet, but Mrs Beard refused to be tempted and shortly afterwards, Christiana left.

If her husband had realised the susceptibility of his female patients, his wife must have been doubly aware of the dangers. She was already suspicious of her husband's new friend and when she later suffered acute pain and sickness, she became convinced Christiana had tried to poison her. Mrs Beard didn't say anything to her husband immediately – the whole idea seemed too far-fetched – but a couple of days later she plucked up courage to confide in him. Dr Beard listened to the account of Christiana's visit, thought it over and went to see her. It was, of course, the perfect excuse to extract himself from an increasingly difficult situation. He told Christiana both he and his wife knew what she had tried to do. He insisted he wanted nothing more to do with her and banned her from his house.

Christiana was enraged. She went home and told her mother she had been accused of trying to murder Dr Beard's wife. It. was impossible anyone could think such a thing of her, she would go mad, she said.

Expecting her mother to be equally shocked, she was horrified when Mrs Edmunds burst into tears and said, "My poor child, you are already mad."

The story came flooding out. For generations there had been cases of dangerous insanity on both sides of the Edmunds family. Christiana's father, the respected architect, had died in Earlswood Asylum when he was only 46. Her sister had tried to throw herself from a window before she died. Her brother had also died in an asylum. Mrs Edmunds' father had died during an epileptic fit, but for years before that he had been out of his mind.

Her mother must have hoped the terrible secret would bring Christiana to her senses, but it seemed to have no effect. Instead, her daughter ranted and raved until Mrs Edmunds agreed to write to Dr Beard threatening to take him to court for slander if he didn't apologise. When he didn't answer, Christiana knew she had to convince him that if there was a poisoner in Brighton, it wasn't her, and she began to put a diabolical plan into action.

She forged letters which allowed her to obtain quantities of arsenic and strychnine from local chemists, supposedly to rid herself of troublesome cats. Then she took her usual afternoon walk. While in the town, she selected one of the impoverished children who roamed the streets and promised him a reward if he ran an errand for her. She gave him money and sent him to a well-known confectioners for a bag of chocolate creams, telling him to return to her as quickly as possible. When he had done as he was instructed and received his small reward, Christiana sent him on his way and carried her prize back to Gloucester Place and into her bedroom. Carefully, she eased each sweet open and added a dose of poison to the filling. While out for her walk a couple of days later, she stopped another child and gave him the bag of sweets, telling him to return them to the confectioners and exchange them for smaller ones.

The plan fell into place with cruel ease. The shopkeeper happily substituted the poisoned chocolate creams for smaller ones and the child took them back for his reward. Encouraged, Christiana repeated the exercise with equal success and almost immediately achieved her aim. Several people became suddenly and mysteriously ill.

One, a little boy of only four years old called Sidney Albert Barker, died 20 minutes after eating a chocolate cream which had been bought for him by his uncle.

Christiana herself took the stand at the child's .inquest and made a statement saying she knew of others who had eaten sweets purchased at the confectioners in question and who had become ill as a result. The shopkeeper roundly denied selling dangerous goods and assured the court that he had now burnt his entire stock of chocolates. Knowing the events must be publicised, Christiana insisted she had warned the local police there was a poisoner in the town and accused them of stupidity. The press eagerly took the bait and she became a star.

But Dr Beard remained silent.

Soon, seemingly at random, parcels began arriving at homes about the town. In them were cakes, sweets and fruit and with them came anonymous notes. One that later came to light said: 'A few home-made cakes for the children. Those done up are flavoured on purpose for yourself to enjoy. You will guess who this is from. I can't mystify you, I fear. I hope this will arrive for you tonight while the eatables are fresh.'

Many of the people who received the gifts were stricken by sudden illness and the police were baffled. Some of the parcels were posted locally, but others had come from London. Christiana, still the heroine, marched into the Town Hall and called the police idiots. She made a public demand that they take action to save Brighton's innocent residents and that is exactly what they did.

On August 17th 1871, George White, Brighton's Chief Constable, put an announcement in the local paper asking for information leading to the capture of the poisoner. He offered a reward of £20. Dr Beard and the chemists who had supplied Christiana with the poison read the piece and took their suspicions to the police. The forgeries she had used to obtain arsenic and strychnine were laid alongside the notes which had been found in the parcels and the handwriting was compared.

Christiana's downfall was imminent. Only two days later, she appeared before magistrates charged with the attempted murder of Mrs Beard.

In the weeks that followed the evidence against her mounted. Dr Beard told the court his story. The children she had made her unwitting accomplices came forward. The chemists gave their testimony. By the time Christiana was committed for trial at the Lewes Winter Assizes, the charge of murdering Sidney Barker had been added to that of attempted murder.

Christiana had become a local heroine in her stand for justice, but scandal now made her star shine brighter than ever. Through it all, she remained totally calm and unrepentant. She was shown a copy of pen-

and-ink portraits of her which were selling in the streets and her only reaction was that it didn't do her justice.

Her notoriety was such that she was eventually brought before a Judge at the Old Bailey in London. The case was handled with great care. Christiana's mother took the stand, pouring out the family history to a rapt audience and the lawyer for the defence asked for leniency on grounds of insanity. Despite this, the jury returned a verdict of guilty.

When asked if she had anything to say, Christiana responded, "It is owing to my having been Dr Beard's patient that I have been brought into this position. I wish the jury could have known the exact particulars of his intimacy with me and the way I have been treated."

And she took one last act of revenge, she announced to the court that she was pregnant.

Sentence was delayed until the truth of her statement could be judged. When it was found to be false, Christiana Edmunds was sentenced to death.

The Brighton newspapers were overjoyed, but the national papers took a more compassionate view. The *Daily Telegraph* commented:

"If this wretched, half-crazed creature, the sister, daughter, and grandchild of lunatics, is put out of the world in deference to a judicial definition of the plea of insanity, her death will bring disgrace upon British justice."

Christiana's Judge, Sir Samuel Martin, applied to the Home Secretary who, in turn, applied to the Queen. The sentence was commuted and Christiana spent the rest of her life in Broadmoor. She died at the age of 78. A murderer, certainly, but also to some extent, a victim. ❏

SARAH ANN FRENCH

(d. 1852)

THE ONION PIE MURDERER

CERTIFIED COPY of an   ENTRY OF DEATH
Pursuant to the Births and   Deaths Registration Act 1953

HC 052953

Registration District   *Lewes*

1852. Death in the Sub-district of   *Lewes*   in the   *County of Sussex*

No.	When and where died	Name and surname	Sex	Age	Occupation	Cause of death	Signature, description, and residence of informant	When registered	Signature of registrar
7	Tenth April 1852 At the Gaol All Saints	Sarah Ann French	Female	27 years	Wife of William French Labourer (Deceased)	Hanging Not certified	John Sanders Occupier County Gaol Lewes	Fourth May 1852	John Gother *Registrar*

Certified to be a true copy of an entry in a register in my custody.

...... *J Beattie* ....Superintendent Registrar
.....................18 August 1987.....Date

In the previous chapter, you will find the story of the chocolate cream murderer. Here we record another diabolical culinary delight hidden beneath the crust of an onion pie. The village of Chiddingly, where this sordid event took place, is set back from modern intrusions like main roads and superstores. You can easily imagine yourself back in the last century as you pass old cottages and farm gates. So little has the 20th century intruded that television companies often come to the village to film period productions free from electricity pylons and telegraph poles.

In this atmosphere you can almost see 35-year old William French walking home to his wife and little boy on the Christmas Eve of 1851 after a hard day spent threshing at Stream Farm. Working with him had been a fellow farm labourer named William Funnell and as the two men chatted before going home, French mentioned the onion pie his wife had promised to bake him. He had been looking forward to it all day.

When he reached home, French found his wife had a visitor, James Hickman, the young man who was courting Sarah's sister. Hickman was often at the Frenchs' home – a circumstance which didn't please William French. On this occasion, however, hunger was more pressing than jealousy and French ignored Hickman and fell upon the onion pie which Sarah had baked for him as promised.

No one else touched the pie and almost immediately after finishing it, French began to feel ill. Agricultural labourers often work on Christmas day, but French didn't go to the farm the following day, nor the day after. When he did go back to work on the third day, he was still being violently sick. He told William Funnell, the onion pie had 'interrupted his inside'.

After several days, French seemed to be improving, but then he was taken ill again. Hickman visited Sarah while her husband was in bed and while he was there he heard French vomiting. He said it didn't sound as if French would live much longer if he was as ill as he seemed. Sarah agreed with him. She went upstairs to check on her husband and when she came down, she mentioned that she had thought of sending for the doctor, but that her husband had told her not to. She asked Hickman to get some brandy from the Gun Inn which was just a few yards up the road. He did as she asked and when he got back, Sarah added the brandy to some hot water and took it upstairs.

Soon afterwards, William French was dead.

An inquest was held at the Gun Inn which returned a verdict of 'Died from natural causes' and French's body was duly buried.

Now villages are gossipy places and a rumour was soon going around that William French's death had not been as natural as had been supposed. The rumour became so rife that it reached the ears of Superintendent Flanagan of the East Sussex Police, who decided to look into the matter further. He took Sarah into custody and arranged with the Coroner to exhume French's body and hold another inquest. French was dug up again and put for safekeeping in the belfry of Chiddingly church.

The second inquest was held at the Six Bells Inn nearby the church. The evidence was put before the jury and Sarah was charged with the wilful murder of her husband. When she was brought to trial at Lewes Assizes on March 20th 1852, the story that unfolded was not a pretty one.

A local woman named Elizabeth Seal testified that she had met Sarah when she was on her way to Hailsham to do some shopping and described a conversation which jokingly implied Sarah wasn't happily married. When they reached Horsebridge, Sarah had gone into the house belonging to the farrier.

Sarah apparently knew the servant there and was introduced to the farrier's wife, Naomi Crowhurst. She asked Mrs Crowhurst if she could buy some arsenic because she was 'just overrun with mice' . Naomi Crowhurst asked Sarah a few questions before she agreed, but ended by putting some arsenic into a packet for her and writing on it the word 'Poison' .

With the arsenic in her possession, Sarah had the means to kill her husband. James Hickman's evidence explained the motive.

Hickman had met Sarah while he had been courting her sister, Jane. He was attracted to Sarah and it was obvious the feeling was mutual. He had often visited her when her husband was out and she had sat on his knee of her own accord and kissed him. She frequently told him she loved him and had asked if he would marry her if she was free. Hickman admitted that he had said he would. One day, she mentioned her husband's illness, saying she thought it might kill him and again asking Hickman if he would marry her if French was dead. Hickman said he saw no signs of death in French and told the court that Sarah had replied, "If you knew as much about it as I do, Jem, you would think there was." She then told him he mustn't tell anyone what she had said.

Apart from a bit of kissing and cuddling, Hickman manages to make his part in the affair sound relatively innocent up to this point. But the contrast is suspiciously great between this statement and his account of what happened only days after French died. *The Times* dated March 22nd, reported Hickman's testimony:

'On the night of the funeral the prisoner began taking her clothes off, and told me to come to bed to her, and I did so. This was the first occasion on which there had been any improper intimacy between us. Her son was in a little bed by the side of the one in which we slept. I remained all night in the house at the request of the prisoner. The prisoner's sister slept in the same bed with us, and she remained in the cottage seven to eight days . . .

In an attempt to defend herself, Sarah made a statement which was read out in court, stating that it had been Hickman who put the poison in the onion pie. She said that when she had complained about her husband staying out late, Hickman had said he had given him something to make him stay out even later. She also said he had been hiding in the house when the

In summing up, Judge Baron Parke told the jury that it made no difference if Sarah actually administered the poison by her own hand, whether she knew of it being administered by any other person, or whether she had asked someone else to administer it. Even if they thought Hickman had administered the poison and that Sarah knew about it or had asked him to do it, in the eyes of the law she would still be guilty of murder.

The jury retired at three-fifteen. When they returned at five o'clock, the foreman said, "We find the prisoner guilty of murder, but some of the jury are of the opinion that the poison may have been administered by some other party, and that the prisoner was only an accessory before the fact." He asked if that made any difference. The Judge replied that it didn't. He pronounced a verdict of Wilful Murder and sentenced Sarah to death. In the public gallery, James Hickman listened without betraying a flicker of emotion.

Later, Sarah made a statement exonerating Hickman and admitting administering the arsenic to her husband. Which of her statements was true? Could Hickman have been carrying on with Sarah for so long and not known what was going on or have any part in it? At one point, Hickman admitted he had been in the house when the police came to arrest her, but that Sarah had pushed him bodily into a cupboard – and yet Hickman was a strapping lad of 20 and Sarah was a petite woman, barely five feet tall. Although several members of the jury were obviously suspicious of Hickman, the police took no further action: they had their murderer and that was good enough for them. Two minutes after noon on April 10th 1852, Easter Saturday, Sarah was led to the gallows before a crowd of 4,000. The bell was already tolling. As she mounted the gallows steps, the executioner covered her head with a white hood. The noose was placed around her neck and the trapdoor was released.

Sarah and William's little boy, a frail child of seven, was put into the workhouse, but was later taken to live with a relative.

A witness who was present at the execution later recorded seeing smiles on many faces among the crowd and hearing laughter. The execution of Sarah Ann French was one of the last public hangings to be held at Lewes. ❑

GUNDRADA
(d.1085)

CONQUEROR'S DAUGHTER? THREE TIMES BURIED

The Tomb-stone of GUNDRAD, Daughter of William the Conqueror, & Wife of William, the first Earl of Warren, which having been deposited over her Remains in the Chapter-house of Lewes Priory, and lately discovered in Iffield Church, was removed to this Place, at the expence of William Burrell Esq.
A.D. 1776.

For someone described while she was alive as a pious woman of very noble character, Gundrada has caused a great deal of controversy since her death. She also has the distinction of having been buried three times.

Gundrada was the wife of William de Warenne of Normandy who came over with Duke William in 1066 and helped him to become the Conqueror. For his services, de Warenne was granted 300 manors in Sussex, Northants, Yorkshire, Norfolk and Suffolk. The most important of these was the Rape of Lewes.

A stronghold already existed at Lewes, but de Warenne added to it, building a stronger fortified castle – the ruin of which still stands over the town – and here he brought his bride in approximately 1070.

Over the years, some very eminent scholars have struggled with the problem of who Gundrada was – particularly, of who her father was.

In *The Worthies of Sussex,* Mark Antony Lower writes: "Gundrada was the fifth daughter of William the Conqueror by his wife, Matilda of Flanders. This statement has been strongly and elaborately contradicted; but there is no reasonable doubt on the subject."

This casual assertion that there can be no reasonable doubt of her being the Conqueror's daughter must have ruffled more historian's feathers than most of us would care to count. The result is a list of possible ancestors and suggestions as to the circumstances of her birth that would need a book of its own to relate. Recent research points to her having come from an illustrious Flemish family, possibly with royal connections. Whoever's daughter she was, the fact remains that William de Warenne's name is rarely mentioned without Gundrada's, indicating that she was an important person in her own right.

When Gundrada and her husband had been living at Lewes Castle for a few years, they decided to make a pilgrimage to Rome. It has been suggested William was feeling guilty about all the Saxons he slaughtered at the Battle of Hastings, but this seems unlikely considering the cruelty of the times when such things would probably have been taken for granted. However, no matter what sparked off their departure, presumably they were making the pilgrimage for the sake of their souls.

They left England in good heart, but were halted by the war in northern Italy and forced to delay their journey in Burgundy. While they were waiting for things to simmer down, they visited the Abbey of Cluny where it seems Gundrada had family connections. During their stay at the monastery, they were so impressed by the discipline and sanctity of the brethren that they resolved to found a Cluniac priory of their own. By the year 1082, one of the most powerful monastic houses in England was in place at Lewes.

Gundrada survived only another three years, dying in childbirth at Castle Acre in Norfolk in 1085. Her body was brought home to Lewes and buried in the chapterhouse of the Priory. William died three years later and was buried by her side.

As far as we know, Gundrada and William stayed where they were for the 450 years until the dissolution of the monasteries. Lewes Priory was looted and the elaborately carved tombstones which had covered their burial places disappeared.

Another 200 years passed. Then, in 1775, Dr Clarke, who was the rector of Buxted, happened to take a close look at a slab of Tournai marble on the table tomb of Edward Shirley in Shirley chapel in Isfield. On the under-side, he saw elaborate carvings edged by perfectly legible lettering which translated:

'Gundred, illustrious branch of a ducal race,
Through England's Church diffused the purest grace;
As Mary pious and as Martha kind,
In her were Faith and Charity combined.
Though Death the part of Martha now receives,
Her Mary's better part for ever lives.
O holy Pancras of her wealth the heir,
In mercy hear the gentle mother's pray'r.
On June's 6th Kalend Nature's struggle came,
And chill'd the life-blood in her tender frame;
Her spirit burst its marble shrine and gave
The fragrance of her virtues to the grave.'*

To the great excitement of historians and archaeologists, Gundrada's tombstone had been found. With the consent of the Shirley family, the stone was taken to the church of St. John the Baptist in Southover, close to the Priory ruins, and was placed in the rectory pew.

This time, just 70 years passed before an even more amazing discovery. In 1845, a cutting was being laid for the Lewes to Brighton railway which crossed the site of the old Priory. Only a few days into the work, the excavators found two small caskets made of lead not far beneath the surface of the ground. Carved on the lids of the caskets were the names 'Wilhelmus' and 'Gundrada'. Before the caskets were taken to Southover church to be placed beneath Gundrada's stone where they now rest, the lids were removed. Inside were found collections of bones gathered together which on examination showed signs of once having been buried in the ground. Perhaps when the Priory was about to be suppressed by Henry Viii's men, someone had removed the bodies and reburied them where they thought they would be safe. Who knows if the story is true, but one man, who was there when the caskets were opened, said he saw Gundrada's golden hair, but as the age-old air was disturbed by the new, it perished before his eyes. ❏

* Mantell's translation.

40

MARTHA GUNN
(1727-1815)
DECORUM CAREFULLY PRESERVED

T here are few names as famous in Brighton as Martha Gunn. Born in 1727, she lived in the town when a transformation was taking place. The fishing village of Brighthelmstone was decaying into history and springing up in its place was a fashionable seaside resort fit for a king.

It was in 1750 that Doctor Richard Russell came to the town and declared sea-water baths an excellent cure for rheumatism. His simple statement would have been considered outrageous by many – sea-bathing was almost unheard of in those days – but it was the start of a celebrated career which earned him the title of 'Doctor Brighton' and it began a flourishing industry which centred around the 'dippers'. Martha Gunn was queen of them all. Very little is known of her early life and by the time her name began to appear in the annals of the day, she was already a successful business woman, courted by gentry and commoners alike and described fondly as 'round as a dumpling' .

She made a notable figure on the foreshore, dressed always in black or grey, a substantial matching bonnet secured against the sea breezes, her dress protected by a full white apron. At six o'clock every morning she was in position with her bathing-machines awaiting her first customer. The Brighton ladies would eventually arrive and disappear inside the wheeled huts. Once stays had been unlaced and countless petticoats removed, well-behaved horses would tow the machines down the stony beach and wade into the sea. The ladies trod fearfully down the steps to be taken into Martha's arms and ducked under the waves. Bathers testing the water without taking advantage of the bathing-machines incurred a £5 fine. The sexes were segregated and decorum was carefully preserved, although it has been said that Martha wasn't above making a little extra cash on the side. It wouldn't have been too difficult to arrange the occasional jaunt into the sea by the more flighty ladies and to allow young bucks within telescope range.

An anonymous poet wrote:

'There's plenty of dippers and jockers,
And salt-water rigs for your fun;
The King of them all is "Old Smoaker,"
The Queen of'em "Old Martha Gunn."
The ladies walk out in the morn,
To taste of the salt-water breeze;
They ask if the water is warm,
Says Martha, "Yes, Ma'am, if you please."
Then away to the machines they run
Tis surprising how soon they get stripped;
I oft wish myself Martha Gunn,
Just to see the young ladies get dipped.'

Old Smoaker was the man who operated the men's machines and who was said to have dipped the Prince Regent. By this time, the Prince had built his oriental fantasy in the Steine, and Martha was a frequent visitor to the Royal kitchens where several of her friends were employed. The extravagance of the Pavilion itself was matched by the food stocks in its pantries and she was accustomed to picking up a little perk here and there.

One day, just as she was slipping a pat of butter into the pocket of her voluminous skirts, the Prince walked in and caught sight of her. He made no comment, but engaged her in conversation, all the while edging her nearer and nearer to the huge cooking range. To Martha's horror and the Prince's amusement, she soon found herself standing in a puddle of melted butter. Martha Gunn was still at work in her eighties, no longer dipping bathers herself, but supervising from the shore. She died on May 2nd 1815 when she was 88 years old. A huge crowd turned out for her funeral and the procession was headed by 40 of her colleagues from the beach. She was buried in the old parish church of St. Nicholas in Brighton and her headstone states simply, 'Martha Gunn, bather in the town for nearly seventy years'. ❏

PHOEBE HESSEL
(1713-1821)

BRIGHTON'S AMAZON

If Phoebe Hessel were alive today, she would no doubt enjoy a good laugh at the controversy she has caused. She has been affectionately called Brighton's Amazon, but what was she? A devoted lover, a heroine or an opportunist? The tombstone that stands in the churchyard of St. Nicholas, Brighton reads:

In Memory of PHOEBE HESSEL who was born at Stepney in the year 1713. She served for many years as a private Soldier in the 5th Regt. of foot in different parts of Europe and in the year 1745 fought under the command of the DUKE OF CUMBERLAND at the Battle of Fontenoy where she received a Bayonet wound in her arm. Her long life which commenced in the time of QUEEN ANNE extended to the reign of GEORGE IV by whose munificence she received comfort and support in her latter years. She died at Brighton where she had long resided December 12th 1821. Aged 108 years.'

Phoebe's is a romantic story. When she was 15, she met and fell in love with a private in the 2nd Foot. His name was Samuel Golding and his regiment was known as Kirke's Lambs, and, unfortunately for Phoebe, he was just about to be posted to the West Indies.

The area around the Isle of Dogs where Phoebe was born, was a notoriously rough area of London and her young life hadn't been easy. Her birth certificate, on which she is actually called Pheby, lists her father as 'went away' with a note made by the vicar saying, 'The child was taken from the Church before completion of the record.'

Far from being discouraged by her lover's imminent departure, Phoebe took the opportunity to keep her heart intact and at the same time escape her less than comfortable surroundings. She cut her hair, dressed herself as a man and enlisted in another regiment heading for the West Indies, the 5th Foot. For five years, she and her lover served their country, their regiments sometimes together, sometimes apart, fighting where the need arose, wherever they were sent. In 1745, Phoebe was with the Duke of Cumberland's armies at the battle of Fontenoy when she suffered a bayonet wound in her elbow. She recovered well, still without revealing her sex , and followed her regiment to Gibraltar where Sam was stationed. The lovers weren't together for long, though. Sam was wounded in action, sent home to England and admitted to Plymouth hospital.

With Sam seriously ill, Phoebe couldn't keep her secret any longer. She went to her Colonel's wife, told the whole story and was given a discharge and letters of introduction to Sam's hospital. She went immediately to his bedside and gradually nursed him back to health.

As in all the best love stories, Phoebe and Sam were married and lived happily ever after. Or at least, they were married for 20 years before Sam died and although they were happy together, they also experienced great sadness. They had nine children, but the only one who survived into adulthood joined the navy and was never heard of again.

Alone, Phoebe went to live in Brighton where she met and married William Hessel, a local fisherman. She made a bare living by selling fish, and whatever else she could come by, and she made a good number of friends. By day she would sit at the bottom of Marine Parade dressed in brown serge and a black cloak, half concealed by shawls, and offer apples, sweets and gingerbread from a basket. By night she would sit in the local tap room and peddle her stories. After William died, she was in and out of the poor-house, but even then she was becoming famous. Eventually, she was invited to public functions where she sat in a prominent position next to the Vicar of Brighton. The Prince Regent heard of her exploits, called her a brave soldier and a jolly old fellow and awarded her a pension of half a guinea a week. It's said he offered her a full guinea, but that she declined saying half was sufficient for her needs. When she was 107 and quite blind, she was taken in an official carriage to the local celebrations honouring the Prince's coronation as George IV.

The story of Phoebe Hessel is a wonderful tale and perhaps that is all it is, a fabrication, a fantasy, a jolly good yarn. For years after she died, Phoebe's story was told and retold in newspapers, magazines and books, possibly even inspiring the popular song Polly Oliver. No one questioned its truth. Everyone was happy to be dazzled by the Brighton Amazon. In the early 1790s, she was even credited with helping the police to bring a young robber called Rook to justice and the gibbet.

But the fantasy couldn't last. Enquiring minds delved into army records and made calculations. Phoebe couldn't have been at Fontenoy, they said, because her regiment was stationed in Ireland when the battle was fought and Sam couldn't have been wounded in action in Gibraltar because there was no action there at the time, In fact, the lovers' regiments were never in the same place at any time relevant to Phoebe's tale.

Was she a heroine or a con artist with glib tongue, a gallant soldier or simply an old woman whose memories became muddled in the telling? When she was 106 and in the workhouse again, she still had round cheeks and a deep, strong voice. Impatient with her circumstances, she complained, "Other people die and I cannot." But when she was reminded of her time in the army and asked if she had ever revealed her true sex in all those years, she said, "I told my secret to the ground. I dug a hole that would hold a gallon, and whispered it there."

What is there to say about Phoebe that hasn't already been said, and said with some heat? One thing is sure, true or false, she told a great story. ❑

SOPHIA JEX-BLAKE
(1840 – 1912)

PIONEER MEDICAL WOMAN

by Robert B. McNeil

In 1869, a bitter struggle for the acceptance of women in medicine began in Edinburgh. The protagonist was a lady whose vision and perseverance won through after a campaign lasting almost nine years. Born in Hastings in 1840, Sophia Louisa Jex-Blake was the youngest daughter of Thomas and Maria Jex-Blake, a Norfolk family whose lineage is recorded in Burke's *Landed Gentry*.

Intelligent and independently-minded, Sophia grew up with the intention of spending a career in teaching, like her brother Thomas who went on to become the headmaster of Rugby. After completing her education at Edinburgh in 1861, she spent a year as a teacher in Mannheim in Germany, then in 1865 she travelled to America to visit schools in the Boston area. There she was introduced to Dr Lucy Sewall,

Resident Physician to the New England Hospital for Women and Children.

Sophia was immediately intrigued by medicine, and delighted that Dr Sewall, a fully qualified practitioner, had been able to take up and follow the profession. A friendship began between the two women that was to endure for the rest of their lives. Dr Sewall's work gave Sophia a new ambition and purpose – she made up her mind that she, too, would pursue a career in medicine. After spending a further two years in Boston she returned to Britain resolved to gain a medical degree.

In 1869 Sophia joined a group of other like-minded women and started to canvas various universities. They succeeded on October 29th, when Sophia and seven others became the first women accepted to study medicine in Britain when they were granted admission to the University of Edinburgh Medical School.

This preserve of male supremacy, however, was not yet ready to accord women complete equality of status. The Senatus – the professional group in charge of the curriculum – decided that, while it was all right for the women to study medicine, this itself did not carry the right to a degree – the prerequisite to enable graduates to practise as doctors.

Furthermore, some professors made it clear that they considered it 'indelicate' to teach, simultaneously, both sexes in certain subjects. This was a decision that denied women access to many of the classes. Sophia and the other women found another barrier when they were forced to forego the practical experience of undergraduate 'rounds' of hospital wards at the Royal Infirmary. This was at first restricted, and then for-bidden them.

In 1870, the women endured more humiliation when a group of male undergraduates began harassing them as they entered and left classes. The incident became known as 'the riot at Surgeons' Hall.'

Details of the episode can be found in a letter addressed by an undergraduate to a friend of Sophia's. It shows that not all male students – as indeed not all professors – were against the women's cause. 'Dear Miss Pechey, (the letter began) I wish to warn you, and through you, your friends, that you are to be mobbed again on Monday. A regular conspiracy has been, I fear, set on foot for that purpose. I wish to tell your friends that although the projected demonstration against you on Monday is intended to be much more serious than the one on Friday, and to frighten you all away, you need not in the least fear it. I have made what I hope to be sufficient arrangements for your protection. I have passed the word around among a lot of my friends – not wholly inexperienced in the kind of work – and you will be all right.

During the remainder of term the women continued to brave dissenters and gradually, with the help of the more liberally-minded male students, the demonstrations petered out.

On January 2nd 1871, Sophia made an impassioned speech at a meeting for support to be re-admitted to the Royal Infirmary. Many in the community extended their wholehearted backing – the Lord Provost of the city among them. The application was defeated, however, by a narrow majority of six votes (94 to 88).

Nonetheless, the women's bravery and determination gathered encouragement from many quarters. The Scotsman editor, Alexander Russel, gave Sophia access to the paper's columns, where her eloquent reasoning won much public support. Many professors, too, voiced dismay at the entrenched position taken by some of their colleagues. One professor, J S Blackie, wrote: 'I was deeply saddened by all I heard at the Infirmary meeting last week. May I go as far as to say I am ashamed of my sex.' Another professor, David Masson, stood foursquare with the women throughout their fight, giving full support and advocacy to their cause.

This pressure, combined with the unremitting efforts of Sophia and the other women, paid off on January 1st the following year. At a further meeting held then, the women gained a majority vote (177 to 168), and were readmitted to the Infirmary.

Sophia's next step was to take legal action against the Senatus. She moved for equality of medical tuition and the right to a degree on qualification. The Court found for her in agreeing access to the full curriculum with equal rights and privileges, but left unresolved the question of degree entitlement at the end of the course.

This left Sophia with only one option – to take her case to Parliament. A Bill was taken to London which contained 65 petitions in favour of enabling full degree status. At Westminster, however, 'pressure of other business' made it impossible to fix a date for the vote, and the Bill was shelved until the following year.

In the meantime, Edith Pechey, Sophia's undergraduate friend at Edinburgh, had been advised that it was possible for women to obtain a degree without hindrance at the Medical University in Berne, Switzerland. She took this advice and wrote to tell Sophia. Sophia made the decision to join her in Berne, and there, on January 13th 1877, she gained her MD.

The following year, Parliament finally passed the Bill Sophia had worked so hard to realise. On January 14th 1878, 'A Charter admitting Women to All Degrees' was carried by a majority of 241 to 132.

A few months later, Dr Sophia Jex-Blake returned to Edinburgh where she opened a dispensary for poor women at Manor Place. In 1899, the

Edinburgh Hospital for Women and Children, as it was then known, transferred to her home in Bruntsfield Lodge on the south side of the city. Sophia retired from practice a short time later, 30 years after her quest for equality had begun. In 1911, Bruntsfield Hospital was built on the site of Bruntsfleld Lodge.

Dr Sophia Jex-Blake died at Mark Cross in Sussex on January 7th 1912 and is buried in the churchyard there. At Bruntsfield Hospital a memorial plaque records her unique contribution to the advancement of women in medicine:

'In affectionate remembrance of Sophia Jex-Blake, Founder of this Hospital, to whose large courage, insight and constancy the admission of Women to the Profession of Medicine in this Country is mainly due.' ❑

SHEILA KAYE-SMITH
(1887-1956)

WHAT THOMAS HARDY DID FOR WESSEX, SHEILA DID FOR SUSSEX

by Brian Graebe, Chamnan of the Sheila Kaye-Smith Society

W hen Sheila Kaye-Smith died suddenly in 1956, she had achieved such acclaim, both in this country and in America, that the obituary in the New York Times was able to say, "Sheila Kaye-Smith is to Sussex what Hardy is to his beloved Wessex."

Yet, while Hardy is still in print and widely read, Sheila Kaye-Smith's works are largely confined to the reserve sections of our libraries – though two are still in print, thanks to Virago.

Sheila Kaye-Smith is the true 'regional novelist' of Sussex. During 50 years of steady writing, she had 47 novels published, mostly set in the Sussex she loved. Most of her poems were also set here and, during this long and intense period of activity, she also produced a continuous stream

51

of magazine and newspaper articles about her attitude to life as a Sussex writer.

In 1987, a small band of enthusiasts formed a society to remedy the state of affairs which had relegated Kaye-Smith to the back shelves. Little realising the fascination and the enigma which would captivate their interest in the following years, the first thing that struck home was the lack of interest shown by her own home town of Hastings. One explanation for this could be Sheila's dislike of the 'city red' – from childhood, she had felt the lure of the countryside which surrounded her home in nearby St. Leonards Also the publication in 1919 of *Tamarisk Town,* a fascinating picture of Marlingate (a thinly disguised Hastings) with all the intrigues of the early developers of the growing resort, may not have endeared her to everyone.

Sheila Kaye-Smith was born in 1887 in St. Leonards-on-Sea, the daughter of a devoted local doctor who had recently moved from a practice in Battle. With Mona, the sister two years her junior, she grew up in a typical Victorian home with its complement of governesses, cooks, maids and other servants.

"In the spirit of the times", Sheila wrote, "the new house in Dane Road . . . was built at a time when servants were cheaper and neighbours dearer . . . with a huge cavernous basement to be the prison house of cooks, and a soaring palatial staircase to be the toil and destruction of housemaids."

In her autobiography, published in 1937, Sheila gives us some captivating glimpses of the middle-class St. Leonards of her day, but she draws an even stronger picture in *The Children's Summer* and *Selina Is Older* published earlier in the same decade. The portrayal of Selina and Moira growing-up is a reflection of Sheila's and her sister's childhood. The life and times, the proscriptions and taboos of the late 19th century, and the sense of fun of simpler days are recaptured. Many of the places Sheila describes are still there – the Marwick Gardens, the forbidden flower-beds and the cottage from which the character Foggy would appear to prevent their destruction, the door from which trooped the girls of Ladies' College on their way to tennis practice on the lower lawns, most of all the fragile-looking summer-house with its gilded weathercock.

In *The Children's Summer,* we glimpse most clearly the developing Sheila and the call of the countryside where she wrote about her ambition to 'always live in the country'. Just outside Hastings, on the road from Westfield to Sedlescombe, and still there today, is a farm and oast called Platnix. It was at Platnix that Sheila and her sister were deposited for several months every summer, in the care of the farmer's wife, while their parents enjoyed their annual sojourn in Switzerland.

Sheila Kaye-Smith has often been described as an enigma, largely because, to the chagrin of some Sussex purists, her works contain actual place-names and locations, but also a name or place just because they appealed to her, in which case, she felt entitled to move them around. But the point is that underlying these literary devices is a convincing and accurate picture of a closely observed scene. The life of the country labourer and the frustrations of rural life, the corn laws and the effect of enclosure acts are incorporated into romances of all sorts, all in her beloved Sussex.

Sometimes, it's true, her stories stray across the border into Kent – to places like the Isles of Oxney and Ebony – for Sheila said, 'East Sussex is far more like West Kent than it is like West Sussex.'

As a developing writer, Sheila Kaye-Smith was hard at work long before her first novel appeared in 1908. At a very tender age, she would walk around her St. Leonards home reciting whole books – stories she had composed in her head and knew by heart. Later came the little penny notebooks in which she wrote quite long Sussex stories with fascinating titles like, *Northward of Brede, The Rector of Daiington, The Gallants of Imberhow* and many more. In fact, a dozen of these unpublished childhood stories and poems still exist in an American archive and no doubt would be of absorbing interest if access could be gained.

As well as novels and poems, Sheila had several plays published. Two, written in Sussex dialect, were called *The Shepherd of Lattenden* and *The Child Born at the Plough*. The latter is a simple nativity play set around the Plough Inn at Udimore and a number of the characters have local names like Leasan, Wickham and Slinches. It has been noted that Sheila was already earmarking the very spot in the Sussex countryside where she would eventually settle. Over half her life was spent in her native Hastings and many would claim that her best works were written in the little room at the top of 9 Dane Road.

Sheila went through a period of groping with life and its meaning. Attracted to the high church style of worship practised at nearby Christ Church, she was entranced by its mystery and its winking lights. Her parents were not entirely of this mould, but they gave her freedom and encouragement. However, after her years at St. Leonards Ladies' College and her breakthrough into writing, she went through periods of disillusionment and for a time became an ardent atheist.

For a while she moved around within the London literary scene, meeting most of the noted writers of the day. But she was never entirely happy or at ease and often took the opportunity to go home to the South Coast. The war years saw her busy in London working in the War Office and engaged in making bandages – at the same time exploring London church life and finding her way back to her faith.

In Hastings after the war, she returned to her beloved Christ Church, and then came an intriguing event which was to change her life. We know little of Sheila's love life, but after several unhappy affairs, she got to the stage when she said she would marry the first man who asked her! The situation at Christ Church was typical of Anglo-Catholic practice at the time. All its priests were unmarried and dedicated to a celibate life. The Rector, the much loved Father Roberts, was fiercely protective of his curates, but less so with a senior curate called Theodore Penrose Fry. Who proposed, we don't know, but it rather seems Sheila did. At any rate, there was, eventually, a very quiet, before-breakfast wedding at a nearby church and as a result, the newly-wed Frys had to leave Hastings. Penrose became curate of a small church in the slum area of Notting Dale, London, and there Sheila continued her writing. She produced a small, but captivating book Wedding Morn, about life in a poor London area.

But disillusionment returned. As a clergyman's wife, she saw the machinations of church life behind the scenes and in 1929, both she and Penrose were converted to Catholicism.

Scouring the Sussex countryside, they found a tumble-down farm called Little Doucegrove. It had a barn and two oasts at Horns Cross near Northiam, overlooking the valley of the River Tillingham. They set about organising its refurbishment while they honeymooned on the continent. A factor that shaped their lives at this point was their discovery of a Normandy saint called Teresa of Lisieux, popularly known as 'Little Flower', who was canonised in 1925. Saint Teresa proclaimed a simple faith of trust and abandonment which appealed to Sheila and Penrose. Shortly after moving into their oasthouse, they converted a stable-loft into a chapel. They named it the 'Oratory of the Little Flower' and waited to see what would happen. To everyone's surprise, the local folk turned up in such numbers that the floor began to collapse. Unabashed, the Frys erected and financed a permanent church on their land and to this day, the church of St. Teresa of Lisieux remains well attended.

Life went on in these pleasant surroundings, interrupted only by the Second World War when Little Doucegrove found itself well and truly in 'bomb alley'. Vivid recollections of these dangerous days were related in a book published in 1945 called Kitchen Fugue, in which Sheila describe conditions in the countryside and set out typical wartime recipes devised by country folk to overcome food shortages. The book includes many amusing tales of animal life, especially of her cats 'Tuesday' and 'Nikolous Ridikulous – the cat to end all cats.'

Books continued to flow from her pen at an average of about one a year. One book which became especially popular and which is still in print, was *Joanna Godden*, the tale of an intrepid woman farmer on Romney Marsh. The book was made into a successful film of the same name which starred Googie Withers, Jean Kent and John McCallum and included a large cast of locals as extras. When, tragically, Sheila collapsed and fell to her death down the stairs of her oasthouse, there was still a part-completed book on her desk.

Her life had been far from uneventful and involved trips to America to publicise her books and give lecture tours. To the end of her days, Sheila Kaye-Smith was writing and reading on a prodigious scale and still finding time to be more of a clergyman's wife than she had ever been when she was one, for Penrose had had to relinquish his priesthood and was content to assist as a layman in the new church.

Strangely for such regional works, her books found an eager audience in America where sales often equalled or outstripped those in this country. Penrose Fry was completely broken by his wife's sudden death. The house was put up for sale. All her original manuscripts, letters, notes and papers, were sold through an agency and to this day remain in America, mostly in the archives of the University of Texas. ❏

DAME GRACE KIMMINS
(1870-1954)

FOUNDER OF THE GUILD OF THE BRAVE POOR THINGS

In the late 19th century, Juliana Horatia Ewing wrote a novel called, *The Story of a Short Life*. It was the tale of Leonard, a crippled boy who lived in the slums of London, and of how he faced up to the problems of his life and let them '. . . count up to be as brave as having one wound in battle.' The writing held the heavily sentimental style of the day, but Leonard's courage and fighting spirit shone through with far reaching consequences. The story was read by Grace Thyrza Hannam and became the inspiration behind Chailey Heritage.

Grace, the eldest daughter of a cloth merchant, was born in Lewes in 1870. She attended Wilton House School in Reading and there became committed to the Christian ideal of service to the poor. Soon after leaving school, she went to work with underprivileged families in the East End of London and became preoccupied with the plight of disabled children. Apart from the squalid conditions in which most of them lived, Grace realised that one of the saddest aspects of their existence was their loneliness and their feeling of inferiority caused by the need to be totally dependent on others.

The Story of a Short Life changed her perspective.

After discovering the character of Leonard, she began to see all disabled as wounded soldiers fighting the battle for an independent life. On St. Martin's Day in 1894, with the help of her friend, Alice Rennie and a band of influential women like the Duchess of Bedford, Mrs Henry Fawcett and Lady Lunn, she founded the Guild of the Brave Poor Things. In the same year, she founded The Guild of Play cultivating play as an art form , mainly for the benefit of underprivileged girls.

The Guild meetings were first held at Cleveland Hall which was owned by the West London Mission. It then moved to the Bermondsey University Settlement which had been founded by the Wesleyan minister, John Scott Lidgett. Regardless of age or creed, men, women and children with all types of disabilities were coaxed to attend every week and take part in an ever-growing round of activities. To make the hall inviting, Alice filled it with flowers. There was a reading table, lectures were given and handicraft classes were begun. But the essential activity of the afternoons was singing and meetings always ended with the Tug of War Hymn, 'The Son of God goes Forth to War' .

The success of the venture was immediate and the Guild of the Brave Poor Things grew and spread to other areas in the city and to other parts of the country. The Guild's motto, *'Laetus sorte mea'* – Happy in my lot – was familiar to all, but there was no complacency involved and it inspired a new courage and a defiance of failure.

In 1897, Grace married Dr. Charles William Kimmins, a child psychologist, educationist and scientist who for many years was Chief Inspector of London County Council Schools. His experience, advice and support became invaluable to Grace and her cause, although he tended to stay in the background. They lived initially at Harrow-on-the-Hill where they had two sons. It might well have been the sight of her two boys growing up in those pleasant surroundings that led Grace to the next step in her work.

Many of the disabled children suffered from tuberculosis and she knew that they stood little chance of leading useful lives in the grimy streets of London. A residential home was needed, somewhere in the country where the children could breathe clean air – even if only for two weeks a year. She began to make a study of different areas of the country to see which would prove the most beneficial. Her research brought her home to Sussex. At Chailey, she looked over an old farmhouse which had once been used as a workhouse. It was a dilapidated building, the roof was leaking and it was infested with rats, but Grace had the imagination to see beyond such minor drawbacks. And she had an even more interesting idea – why limit the children to a fortnight's holiday? Why not bring them to live there, in an atmosphere where they could grow healthy and strong while learning to work and support themselves? ,

Chailey Heritage was founded in 1903 with £5 in the funds and seven disabled boys. Grace used her tremendous gift for fund-raising to collect enough money to begin work on rebuilding and extending the Heritage and it became the first purpose built school for disabled boys in the country. Five years later, she was able to accommodate girls as well as boys.

Since then, many hundreds of children have come to the Heritage to receive the latest medical treatment and to learn. In the First World War, 590 children suffering from shock brought on by enemy raids were housed there and almost as many wounded soldiers were treated and rehabilitated side by side with the disabled residents. During the Second World War, the care was extended to include the children who fell victim to the Blitz. More recently, Chailey helped many of the victims of thalidomide. In 1948, the Heritage was nationalised with the introduction of the NHS, but it has since been re-formed as a charitable trust.

Grace spent her whole life working for the disabled.

In 1927, she was awarded the CBE and later became a Dame of Grace of the Order of St. John of Jerusalem. In 1950, she was made Dame Commander of the Order of the British Empire. Her younger son, Anthony Kimmins, OBE, described her with deep affection as a dictator. He said she was a woman with enormous drive and personality, a resolute knowledge of what she wanted and a tremendous belief in her own powers.

Her Christian ideals never faltered. At her request, clergymen of all ranks, including Bishops, came to preach at the daily services in the Heritage Chapel – but none were allowed to go on indefinitely, If she thought her Chaplain's sermon had gone on long enough for the disabled children sitting in the pews and for herself, she would signal with a wave of her hand to cut him short. Apparently, she later had a red warning light fitted in the pulpit which she could operate to great effect from her seat at the rear of the Chapel.

Dame Grace Kimmins died in 1954. In the years since her death, several people say they have seen Grace walking the Heritage grounds. No doubt she approves of the work that continues there and of the Chailey Heritage Charter of Children's Rights which was drawn up in 1990. It states that each child has the fundamental right to be valued as an individual, to be treated with dignity and respect, to be loved and cared for as a child first and to be safe. ❏

CHARLOTTE KING
(1867 – 1948)

A TENT IN THE BUSH TO A MANSION IN THE WEALD
by Jasper Ridley

Charlotte Elizabeth Francis was born on 17th October 1867 in a tent in the bush in Queensland, Australia. Her parents, Arthur Morley Francis and wife Angela, had come to Queensland from England in 1861, and had acquired 70 acres of scrub and forest on the banks of the River Brisbane. The property was only nine miles from the town of Brisbane as the crow flies, but the 14 mile journey along the river by canoe could take 24 hours or more when the river was in flood – there was no doctor nearer than Brisbane.

Charlotte nearly died when she was a small child. She fell ill, and would eat nothing except the oysters from the crannies in the rocks on the river bank. Her brothers risked their lives to travel to Brisbane along the flooded river to obtain the light food, medicines and flannel that she needed.

On another occasion, when she was helping her brother Dick to cut wood, he accidentally struck her hand with an axe. They managed to stop the bleeding without the help of a doctor but the wound left a scar which she kept all her life. Dick himself was less lucky when his gun went off accidentally and he lost one of his fingers. When he was still a young man, he died of pneumonia while trying to rescue people in the great Queensland flood of 1893.

Arthur Francis did not make his fortune in Australia. 'We never found gold, or pearls or tin', wrote Angela, 'or became big squatters. We tried to get our living by growing cotton, bananas and Indian corn. These almost all failed.' Arthur became a journalist writing for radical newspapers and, later, a Queensland MIP. The government appointed him a JP and Police Commissioner to keep him quiet. His duty was to ride through a tract of country several hundred miles wide and try to prevent the European squatters from exterminating the native Aborigines.

By the time Charlotte was three, the family had built a log cabin to replace their tent. Charlotte slept in her own room in the cabin. Her parents used to place a glass of water by her cot when she went to bed. One night she noticed a very long snake coming down from a hole in the roof It stretched down and drank the water in the glass and retreated through the hole. Charlotte did not tell anyone, and the next night the snake came again and drank the water. It was only after it had been coming for four or five nights that she happened to mention it to her parents. That night they put her in another room and sat up waiting. The snake duly appeared. It was a deadly Australian Black Snake and Arthur shot it. Charlotte was very sad as she had grown fond of it.

When Charlotte was 25 her cousin, John Godwin King, arrived from England. Both his father and grandfather had been doctors in Everton, Lancashire. The grandfather had been shrewd enough to buy shares in gas companies in the 1840s and had become rich. His son, Godwin's father, later moved to London and bought a 20-room house in Hampstead. Godwin King went to Cambridge and studied medicine, but never practised. He was 28 when he arrived in Queensland in 1892, having travelled previously in the United States, Japan and India. He and Charlotte fell in love. Though Godwin was a Nonconformist, they were married in Brisbane Cathedral to please Charlotte's mother,

The newly wed couple returned to England and went house hunting – they were looking for a suitable gentleman's residence in the country anywhere in the South of England. They nearly bought a house in Hampshire, but the deal fell through at the last moment. In March 1896, they bought Stonelands, a mile from the village of West Hoathly near East Grinstead. Part of the 13-room house was a stone building dating from

1560, but in 1875 a previous owner had added a wing in redbrick for the servants' quarters. There was a ten acre garden, about 100 acres of farmland, as well as woodland and a stone quarry. The property cost £9,200. The couple added another wing to the three storey house with an additional eight rooms. It was built with stone from the quarry on their property and the total labour cost for the new addition was £400.

They also built coach houses and stables, cowsheds, pigsties and barns for the farm, and cottages for their labourers. A new West Drive was also laid out, in addition to the main East Drive and the Farm Drive, and a lodge was built at the entrance to each. In all there were nine semi-detached cottages on the estate. They employed five women servants in the house – a cook at £40 a year and a parlourmaid, a housemaid, a kitchenmaid and a scullerymaid at £25 a year each, plus their food and lodging. A coachman, a gardener and four other men who worked on the farm lived in the cottages on the estate. It was not long before the coachman became the chauffeur, for Godwin was one of the first motorists in Sussex. He drove himself, but Charlotte was driven in the second car by the chauffeur.

So Charlotte had moved within a few years from a log cabin in Queensland to a 21-room house in Sussex. A year after they bought Stonelands, she gave birth to her first child, a daughter whom they named Ursula. When Charlotte's father died in Queensland, she and Godwin went there with their four year old Ursula, to sell the log-cabin and bring Charlotte's mother back to England. She lived with them at Stonelands until she died.

Although Charlotte, at 29, became the mistress of Stonelands, she was the odd woman out among the wives of the West Hoathly gentry. There were more than a dozen other houses with 20 rooms, long drives, large gardens, farms, woodlands and cottages within a few miles; but the owners were all Conservative Party members and attended the Church of England service every Sunday at the parish church in the village. Godwin was a mixture of Nonconformist and Freethinker, and Charlotte was a Unitarian. They were both ardent Liberals and believed that the Church of England was the Tory Party at prayer – the same Tory Party that had persecuted Nonconformists under Charles II, had opposed the abolition of the slave trade, and was now pursuing a jingoistic imperialist policy in Africa. They did not go to church or to the Countess of Huntingdon chapel and Ursula was not baptised.

Godwin's brother Joseph King was elected as the Liberal MP for North Somerset in 1910. Godwin refused invitations to stand for Parliament as a Liberal candidate, but was elected to the Sussex County Council in 1899 as an Independent. A few years later, he was appointed an Alderman, and remained on the County Council for 49 years until his death.

Despite their political disagreements, they remained on very friendly terms with their Conservative neighbours, except during the bitter election campaigns which followed Lloyd George's 'People's Budget' in 1909 and which led to the abolition of the House of Lords' veto. Godwin and Charlotte had been invited to dinner by the Locker-Lampsons at Rowfant House; but Charlotte received a note from Mrs Locker-Lampson withdrawing the invitation as she regretted that she could no longer retain social relations with Liberals.

During the First World War, Charlotte and Ursula worked hard on the farm to help the war effort until Ursula went to work in a munitions factory in East London. But, during the war, Ursula became a Pacifist and a member of the Labour Party. In the inter-war years, she worked actively in the East Grinstead constituency for the Labour candidate; all the elections, however, were won by the Conservative, Sir Henry Cautley, with large majorities. Godwin and Charlotte worked for the Liberal candidate, but remained on friendly terms with their Socialist daughter and indeed with Sir Henry Cautley, who sat with Godwin as a JP at the East Sussex Quarter Sessions.

Charlotte was one of the founder members of the Women's Institute in 1915, becoming chairman of her local branch. But her greatest interest was in producing plays. In 1909, she attended the University Extension lectures at Oxford given during the summer vacation by Gilbert Murray. He had translated the plays of the ancient Greek dramatists Euripides, Sophocles and Aeschylus into English rhyming verse. The translations have been sharply criticised by experts, but they became best sellers in Edwardian England. Charlotte decided to produce them for amateur actors in the village.

Her first production, *The Trojan Women,* with Charlotte as Hecuba, was performed on the terrace of Stonelands in 1910. Next year they did *Hippolytus;* her parlourmaid played the leading role of Phaedra, and Charlotte the supporting part of the old Nurse. In 1912, they moved from the terrace to the 16th century barn in the farmyard at Stonelands and a Greek play continued to be performed there every summer, except in wartime, until 1936.

Charlotte's daughter, son-in-law, grandson and friends were all enlisted to play the parts and so were the villagers. The chauffeur always played a leading role, and the village women were the Chorus. Gilbert Murray, who became a close friend of Charlotte's, came to watch the plays and waived his royalties. A high standard of amateur acting was always displayed, but Charlotte refused to allow the actors to take a bow at the

62

end or for their names to be printed on the programmes. This would have encouraged vanity.

Godwin did not approve of the theatre – his Nonconformist ancestors had condemned it. He never went to the theatre in London, but made no attempt to discourage Charlotte from going, which she often did. He also strongly disapproved of make-up. Charlotte was equally opposed to make-up in ordinary life – she never wore any, and never dressed fashionably. But she thought it was justifiable in the plays to use eye make-up and for the men to wear false beards.

When Charlotte performed the plays at the barn, Godwin stood in the drive telling the audience where to park their cars, and then slipped into the barn to watch the play from a special seat reserved for him at the side, away from the rest of the audience. There were usually four performances every year, with an audience of about 150 for each performance. Admission was free, though there was a collection to defray expenses. Many of the village people came to watch the plays. In 1910, there was no other entertainment in the village, and the villagers enjoyed seeing their relatives and friends acting. Charlotte called her company 'The Stoneland Players'. It still performs plays today,

In performing the devastating tragedies of more than 2,000 years ago, Charlotte found consolation for the personal tragedies in her own life. Her second child, Phoebe, died of chickenpox in 1906 when she was 13 months old. Her only other child, Ursula, developed *retinitis pigmentosa* when she was a teenager. It did not immediately affect her eyesight enough to prevent her from enjoying her favourite hobby of painting, but she was nearly blind by the time she was 50. Before Charlotte died, it had become an accepted truth that cousins should not marry, as it increased the chances of the recurrence of rare hereditary diseases. She and Godwin blamed themselves for their daughter's blindness, all the more because their marriage had been so happy.

They were saddened by the changes in the modern world. They bought and restored the 17th century manor house in West Hoathly and gave it to Ursula when she married. At first she and her husband lived there with three women servants in the house and a chauffeur and gardener in the cottages, but after the Depression of 1931, they had to get rid of all the servants except the chauffeur. Charlotte was taken aback when she visited Ursula at the Manor House and Ursula herself opened the door – her mother did not think that this was right. She was even more distressed when Ursula followed the fashion of the day in the 1920s and wore short skirts and painted her face with lipstick like Jezebel. Worse was to come. Ursula and her husband separated, and eventually divorced. Her parents believed that a marriage should be for life and each should be totally faithful to the other.

Charlotte was also saddened by the destruction of the moral values of 19th century humanitarianism and liberalism. She was shocked by the failure of the League of Nations to prevent war, by the persecution of the Jews in Nazi Germany and by the horrors of the Second World War. In 1940, the army requisitioned half the house at Stonelands and the barn and the farm buildings. Godwin and Charlotte lived in the other half of the house with the cook as their only remaining domestic servant although the chauffeur was still an emp[oyee and lived in one of the cottages. He no longer drove Charlotte in the car, for with petrol rationed she usually walked to the village, two miles there and back, even though she was in her late 70s, to sell produce from her garden for the Women's Institute. She kept rabbits at Stonelands, and fed them herself, in order to supplement the rations for her family and the people in the village, who had always loved her.

She lived to see the end of the war and perform the very topical *The Trojan Women* again in 1946. Godwin died in his sleep, aged 84, in February 1948. Charlotte, who was 80, lived on alone at Stonelands with the cook for another four months, but at the end of June she had a stroke. The cook died of a heart attack the same night. Charlotte survived for 11 days, and died with her daughter and grandson at her bedside on July 9th - she would have gone on for years if Godwin had still needed her.

She had always disapproved of funerals and of making a fuss about death. At her express request, her daughter and grandson did not go to Brighton when her body was taken there to be cremated – she did not realise how much their absence from the funeral would be condemned in the village. Her ashes were placed in the grave in the woods at Stonelands with the ashes of her mother, her daughter Phoebe and Godwin. Ursula's ashes were also placed there when she died in 1974. ❑

PENELOPE LAWRENCE
(1856-1932)
DOROTHY LAWRENCE
(1860-1933)
MILLICENT LAWRENCE
(1863-1925)

THE FIRM' THAT STARTED ROEDEAN

In 1895, an idea which was to become a British institution began to take shape in the minds of three sisters. Now a familiar sight, the dignified edifice of Roedean School, on the coast road to the east of Brighton appears to have been there for centuries. One of the foremost independent schools in the country, it stands high on the chalk cliffs overlooking the Channel, as impressive as the story of its founders, Dorothy, Penelope and Millicent Lawrence – 'The Firm'.

Philip Henry Lawrence was born in Liverpool. After he left school, he moved to London to become a solicitor and while he was there, he met and married Charlotte Augusta Bailey. It was a tragically short marriage and in the February of 1857, less than three months after giving birth to her daughter Penelope, Charlotte died.

Some 18 months later, Philip married again. His second wife, Margaret, the daughter of a London architect, loved children and Penelope became the eldest of what was to be a very large family. The Lawrences went to live at Copse Hill in Wimbledon and there Margaret had four children, Henry, Dorothy, Paul and Millicent. It was a happy home, but Philip was working too hard and a year after Millicent was born, his health began to suffer. On medical advice, he took his wife and children abroad and because the system of education in Germany was much admired, they settled in Freiberg in Saxony. Philip was also interested in mineralogy and the town had a well-known mining school. A local nurse and a governess were engaged and German became the Lawrences' home language,

After about six months, Philip's health had improved sufficiently for him to work again and he began making plans to return to London. Margaret was pregnant by this time and, before he went to England, Philip settled her and the children in Versailles. Penelope went to day school and learnt to speak French. She had a clear, analytical mind and she enjoyed exploring new subjects and putting the knowledge gained to practical use. She also learnt to swim and began to understand the value of physical education. After the twins, Ruth and Sylvia, were born, they all spent the summer at Biarritz before rejoining Philip in Wimbledon. There the family increased again – Agatha, and the second set of twins, Roger and Christabel, were born.

By this time, Philip was solicitor to the Commissioners of H M Works and Public Buildings, but he wasn't particularly happy. He had been thinking for some time he would like to become a barrister and this he set about doing. At the same time, he bought a field in Wimbledon Park and began planning a larger house for his growing family. While Fearegg House was being built, Margaret and the children went to live in Dresden where another daughter, Theresa, was born. The Franco-Prussian war was in progress and it was an exciting time to be growing-up in Europe. Although they were happy in Dresden, they were living in an apartment in the centre of the town and Philip and Margaret decided it would be better to live in the country, they were great believers in a healthy life-style with plenty of fresh air and cold baths – so they moved to Gotha in Thuringia. Penelope was 15 by then and she began training at the local seminary for the Froebel diploma. Philip visited when he could, always encouraging his children's growing interest in music and the arts. In 1872, Maximilian was born.

The family returned to England again, and set up home in the newly built Fearegg House in the spring of 1873. In the following year, Penelope went to Newnham College where she eventually became only the third student to pass the Natural Science Tripos, Class II. Her degree however, was withheld, as Cambridge didn't grant such things to women in those days - she was actually awarded her degree by Trinity College, Dublin. Dorothy stayed at Newnham for a while where she was appointed demonstrator. By this time, her young brothers, Richard and Stephen, had been born and Philip and Margaret's family of 14 children was complete.

 Philip was doing reasonably well at the Bar, but unfortunately not well enough. To keep his family and home, he had to borrow money against the house, When the time came to send Dorothy and Millicent to Newnham, he simply couldn't afford the expense. Penelope did all she could, paying for Millicent's teacher training course at Maria Grey College. The younger children were still being taught at home and Margaret managed to persuade a few friends and neighbours to bring their children to join them. Dorothy, who had spent three years at Bedford College, returned home to Fearegg House and, eventually helped by Millicent, devoted herself to teaching at their small house school.

Then, in 1881, disaster struck. Philip had gone to Cumberland as   counsel in a litigation concerning a fishery. Climbing a rock by the river, he slipped and fell 16 feet, seriously fracturing his pelvis.

With her husband unable to work, Margaret was faced with the problem of how to keep her family and home together. Assisted by Dorothy and Millicent, she set about developing Fearegg House into a full-time school. Penelope helped when she could, but she was teaching at Wimbledon High School by this time. Every available inch of Fearegg House was taken over. With all her charm and energy, Margaret encouraged everyone she could to send their daughters to her school. Boarders were taken and more children came as day girls. For the next four years, with an invalid husband and father to contend with, life at Fearegg House was exhausting for everyone.

It was Dorothy's idea to try something different. She and Millicent talked the problem over and came up with a plan to sell Fearegg House and start a school which wouldn't need to be a home at the same time, but that would still make enough to support the family. They were full of ideas, but they needed more - they needed the experience to put their ideas into practice.

Penelope was on holiday in Madeira and Dorothy immediately wrote to her, setting out their proposal: "it seems to me the only way in which it would be possible for us to keep together, and also the only way in which

It is possible to make any money, for though we could all go out as teachers or governesses, we could none of us, except perhaps you, do more than keep ourselves." Penelope responded by sending a cable saying she was on her way home.

Together, the sisters began their search for a suitable building, but none of the country houses they looked at satisfied them. In the end, they consulted Mrs Martineau, or Aunt Fanny as the girls knew her, and she suggested Brighton - where, she said, she had never known a school to fail.

The sisters weren't particularly enthusiastic to begin with. Brighton seemed too 'fashionable' at the time, but it had the reputation of being a healthy town and they saw health as a main ingredient of a good education. A further search was made and in 1885, they took a house in Lewes Crescent. Their brother, Paul, gave them £50 and their father gave his blessing. Together with some of the younger members of the family, ten pupils were installed - 'six paying and four for show'. The new establishment was given the name Wimbledon House School.

'We wish in the first place,' the sisters wrote, 'to give to physical education and outdoor exercise their due place in every girl's life. Secondly, to train each girl to independence and self-reliance and with that in view to give as much liberty as can be granted with safety. And, thirdly, to supply a sound and careful intellectual training to each girl.'

Wimbledon House School was an immediate success. Millicent was found to have a remarkable capacity for business and a talent for organisation. Dorothy had a quiet effectiveness and a way of bringing out the best in everyone. Penelope had a clear vision for the future and the powerful personality to put that vision into practice.

All three had a sense of humour and a love of fun. They started all manner of societies and clubs for their girls and organised expeditions, picnics and plays - which they frequently took part in themselves. Their school was an extension of their family and into it they poured as much care and love as they had always given to their home-life. Paul Lawrence later wrote: 'The success which attended their enterprise was truly remarkable and resulted in rescuing the family from the impending financial disaster which threatened it. Not only were my sisters from the first able to provide for their own maintenance but also for the maintenance, education and advancement in life of all the younger members of the family and our parents were enabled to spend the rest of their lives in peace and comfort.'

For the next 15 years the school flourished, taking over the houses next door, then moving to even larger premises in Sussex Square. A nearby field was chartered as a games field – to the disgust of other local seminaries for Young Ladies, who called it, 'playing in the open!' The number of pupils at the school rose to 90 and at one time, all eight of the Lawrence sisters were teaching there.

By 1895, Wimbledon House School had once more outgrown the bricks and mortar in which it was housed and the three sisters had to think again. The scheme they devised must have seemed extraordinary to many – if not utterly preposterous. They decided to buy some land and build an entirely new school that would bring it architecturally as well as educationally in line with the great independent schools of the day.

The Marquess of Abergavenny sold them 18 acres of land and the architect, John W. Simpson, was employed to convert the sisters' ideas into an official set of plans. An enormous amount of money was needed and they raised the full amount themselves, securing capital from family and friends, as well as anyone else willing to subscribe to their new venture.

Work began in March 1897. Two years later, Roedean was fully operational with four separate boarding houses linked under one roof and designed to be as much like real homes as possible. By 1906, there were 200 pupils in residence. Each sister made Roedean her life's work. Millicent, always cheerful, often took her girls for long country walks. "Come along," she would say, "we have to live, let us enjoy it and live thoroughly." It was Millicent who organised a system of 'scouts' in the school which helped to inaugurate the Guide movement.

Dorothy, although frequently hampered by ill-health, became responsible for the Chapel which was dedicated by the Bishop of Chichester in 1906. In some ways, she was a second mother to the family and troubles were often brought to her sympathetic ear.

Penelope was the spokeswoman and her strength, vitality and enthusiasm, made her an exciting teacher. Having taken to the water while living in Versailles, she was often seen in the sea, encouraging the stronger swimmers among the girls to join her as she swam from one Brighton pier to the other.

During the First World War, despite having to blackout all the windows facing the sea, they kept the school open. The girls were rallied to knit for the troops and to make walking sticks, splints, crutches and fracture boards during their carpentry lessons. Collections were taken in the Chapel for the wounded.

Determined that the school should continue beyond their individual life-spans, they formed a new Company and in 1920, Roedean became the independent school it is today. The sisters retired together in 1924, but for the rest of their lives continued to keep in close contact with the school and with their girls, past and present. Their vision has never diminished.

Today the greatly extended building is surrounded by a 40 acre estate and is home to 480 students.

Penelope, Dorothy and Millicent Lawrence were not the original pioneers of women's education, but they led the second generation of reform and became both innovative and inspirational teachers. To the staff and girls of Roedean, they will always be 'The Firm'. ❑

VIVIEN, DUCHESS OF LEINSTER
(1920 – 1992)

INDOMITABLE AT KEEPING THE CREDITORS AT BAY
by Anthony Finlay

efore her death in 1992, an elderly, somewhat untidy looking
woman was often seen walking her dog along the streets of
Brighton. Plastic shopping bag in hand, wearing over-long
trousers and sensible flat shoes, she cut a forlorn figure, suggesting a
lifetime of being on the breadline.

In fact she was a member of the aristocracy – she was Vivien, Duchess
of Leinster, wife of Ireland's premier duke.

Her beginnings were humble. Born in Battersea in 1920, Vivien Irene
Felton, fifth daughter of a motor mechanic, left school at 15 to take a
variety of menial jobs. Clearly money was tight in the Felton home but
Vivien did her best to help with the finances, finding employment as a
waitress, a cook and a hairdresser. This source of revenue ended when at
17 she found herself pregnant and hastily married the father of the child,

one George Conner, a salesman of 27. Six weeks after the wedding her only child, a boy, was born.

The couple worked hard trying to make a go of things, but the marriage existed in name only. Vivien tried all her former jobs and some new ones like barmaid, book keeper and short-hand typist. By 1955, she was the manageress of a block of flats in Kensington, while George acted as caretaker cum handyman.

Vivien was now 35 and an attractive, dark-haired, rather sharp-featured woman of average height and build.

Soon after taking up the post of manageress, she began to notice a tall, genteel, well-spoken man whose room was always very untidy, strewn with empty tins and cartons. This mysterious person went by the name of 'Mr FitzGerald', she was informed by the owner of the block. She began to pass the time of day with the elderly (he was 63), but still handsome Mr FitzGerald. When they met, Vivien recalled, "he was so untidy and absent-minded, I thought he was probably a professor."

Soon they began an affair. To Vivien, this man represented everything she had never known: good manners, breeding, an aristocratic bearing and 'a fantastic air of dash and romance'. Although he had no money – he was always broke – Mr FitzGerald had a taste for gracious living. He was never a man to let a little matter of shortage of money cramp his style.

He began wining and dining the new woman in his life. Vivien was swept off her feet. "He introduced me to a world I did not know before – art galleries, concert halls and pink champagne.

George's reaction to his wife's infatuation was laconic; he dismissed it as 'midsummer madness' . But he was mistaken. She left her husband and went to live with Mr FitzGerald. Soon she learned his true identity – in reality he was Edward, 7th Duke of Leinster, the premier duke of all Ireland.

Unfortunately, Edward had lost all his patrimony through an injudicious agreement with a money lender whereby for a down payment and a paltry annual allowance he signed over everything. Gambling and high living had been the 7th Duke's downfall. He had entered into the fateful agreement in an effort to save himself – unsuccessfully as it turned out – from being declared bankrupt.

Vivien was forced to choose between her job and the duke. She chose the duke. For nine years they lived together, unable to marry because at this time neither Edward's third wife, the actress Denise Orme, nor George would grant a divorce. It was a trying time for both of them and a constant struggle to remain solvent. Edward, though an intelligent enough man in other ways, had no financial acumen and little drive;

Vivien in contrast would try her hand at anything to make ends meet and had much more financial sense.

In this period they tried several business ventures which were initially successful; but Edward's lack of support told in the end. Thus a tea-shop cum wool shop at Rye in Sussex appeared to be going well in the early days until Edward's insistence in providing the customers with the best of everything proved to be more than the business could sustain. The couple's own meal was invariably baked beans on toast.

One day an Old Etonian came in to sample the couple's teas. He noticed Edward standing in his usual place – at the sink, washing up.

"Isn't that Eton?" he asked, staring at Edward's old school tie. He agreed that it was. "What's your name? FitzGerald. I don't think I remember that name when I was there."

"Oh, the name was different then. It was Leinster."

After this the shop did big business. People travelled vast distances to see a Duke of the Realm washing dishes. "That's the Duke," whispered customers to each other, "and that dark-haired woman is her ".

However, this period of euphoria was not to last. They were plagued by creditors who quickly found out that they lived above the shop. "I would lie in bed all day with the curtains drawn, in case the creditors saw me," Vivien recalled. "While I was in bed, Fitz used to crawl along the floor between the tea tables to the window every time the door bell rang. Then he would peer through the curtains to see if the caller was friend or foe."

In 1965, her divorce came through finally and as Edward's third wife had died in 1960, they were at last free to marry. About this time Vivien had proved instrumental in enabling Edward to get a discharge from his bankruptcies after 28 years, proving herself a doughty fighter in the courts.

They were married at Brighton Registry Office when Edward was 73 and Vivien 45. They set up their first home as Duke and Duchess of Leinster in Arundel Terrace, opposite Blackrock swimming pool, near the Marina. Having by now abandoned her South London accent for a more 'acceptable' one, Vivien became the driving force behind a number of enterprises intended to improve their impecunious lifestyle.

Edward was always in debt. As a result the couple had to assume an itinerant life, trying to keep one step ahead of the debt collectors by constantly moving from one bed-sit or flat to another, all within the Home Counties, mostly Kent, Surrey and Sussex. With the change of address often came a change of name: one favourite was Gay, first adopted when they were living in Birchington in Kent. This pseudonym was of course an ironical reflection of the actual circumstances under which they lived. They managed to keep a sense of humour despite it all.

Unconventional as the Duke's lifestyle was, his fourth Duchess's in some ways matched it. There was the occasion when the two ate in public straight out of the serving dishes – to show the management they did not care. Shortly after their marriage, Vivien was asked to open a bazaar in Sussex. "It was a very hot day so after a few minutes I took off my hat and when teatime came I sat on the grass and kicked off my shoes," she recalled. "Definitely not the way for a Duchess to conduct herself"

"I think this title business is a lot of bunkum," the Duchess is quoted as saying, but she was not averse to using the title where she perceived there might be advantage, as when she opened an up-market boutique in The Lanes, Brighton, called 'La Duchesse' . Needless to say after an initial period of success her boutique failed.

Despite all the financial worry in her life at this time, Vivien retained her good looks – she was still an attractive woman with a bouffant hairstyle and good figure, able to impart confidence in others with her ability to manage. Life with the 'impecunious Duke', as she referred to him, was difficult; so difficult that she actually left him at one stage and went to live with her son, then aged 33. But like all her enterprises this did not last long and she returned to Fitz, who had threatened suicide.

Edward, not surprisingly, was embittered by the loss of his fortune. But equally upsetting to him was the attitude of his own family to his fourth wife (whom they found hard to accept) and to himself in straitened circumstances. So desperate were they, the pair went on a madcap scheme to raid the stately home of Edward's son, to try and remove a priceless painting which Edward believed rightly belonged to him. True to form this escapade was abortive; the police were called to eject the intruders.

Thanks to Vivien's efforts in the courts, Edward, freed at last from the stigma of bankruptcy, was able to take his seat in the Lords, late in 1975. This was a comparatively happy time for the Duke and Duchess judging from their smiles as they were leaving the House on one of their first visits. All was optimism, as Vivien laughed: "He will talk on animal preservation as he prefers animals to people." Although not renowned for his tributes in public to the wife to whom he owed so much, Edward did speak to the Press on the occasion of his appearance in the Lords: "I am afraid I have never been very good at managing my affairs. It was entirely due to the hard work and efforts of my present wife, Vivien, that I was finally discharged from bankruptcy after many years."

Unfortunately, he was unable to enjoy this new found status – at this time a saga of legal disputes came to a head over a family discretionary trust fund from which Edward and Vivien believed they should have benefited. Family arguments ensued. Worry over the uncertain outcome of this, and the continuing enmity between his wife and his son on top of all his other misfortunes, led to the Duke's suicide by an overdose at St George's Drive, Pimlico. He was 83.

At the time Vivien said: "I am not greatly surprised at his death. He was under a dreadful amount of pressure and deeply depressed about his life."

The hard times continued. When interviewed, Vivien with pathos in her voice, said: "I have no regular income of my own from any source and no home of my own." She was not entitled to any state pension as neither the Duke nor she had paid contributions.

However, Vivien was able to move to a flat at Sloane Avenue Mansions, Chelsea, with financial support from her son and stepson. "Now," she said, "I can settle down to paint and my first portrait will be of my late husband." She continued to seek work and in the late 1970s and early 1980s she secured part-time posts with the Royal Marsden Hospital, Chelsea, and with the charity "Help the Aged" where she proved a successful administrator for the organisation and a kind and generous (considering her means) colleague. Just as she was experiencing a period of comparative calm – she was moving in high circles again, having just been granted the freedom of the City of London – Vivien fell ill. When she was fit to return to the charity work she was told that her post had gone. She had just had her salary raised to £3,000.

As if this was not enough, Vivien found herself at daggers drawn with her late husband's second wife, Rafaelle, over a disputed insurance policy of Edward's, which both ladies claimed (it was taken out when the Duke was married to his second wife). In a memorable book detailing her life with the Duke entitled So Brief a Dream and which published in 1973, Rafaelle had beautifully summed up Edward's character: 'fey, wistful, vulnerable – in this world but not of it.'

In 1987 Vivien went back to live again with her first husband, George Connor in Kensington. Here she was known as the untitled Vivien FitzGerald (or Connor) but in Debrett's peerage she was of course listed as the Dowager Duchess of Leinster.

This was not the end of Vivien's peripatetic life. By 1990, she is once again back in Brighton living in the Marine Parade, opposite the central pier. Still she was not defeated and attempted to earn a little from her hobby of painting. George, aged about 80, was still with her.

Vivien's last home was Arundel Lodge at the other end of Marine Parade. The emphysema from which she had suffered for some time took a turn for the worse and she was taken to the Royal Sussex Hospital where she died in February 1992, a few weeks short of her 72nd birthday.

A fitting tribute to this woman who had had more than her fair share of misfortune was given by a close friend: "The Duchess was full of colour, like a bottle of champagne, always bubbly." The pet dog – her 'reason for living' – which she walked round the Brighton streets was brought to Vivien's bedside and was present when she died. ❏

SAINT LEWINNA
(c.7th century)
THE STORY OF THE STOLEN BONES

So little is known about Saint Lewinna that you might wonder why she is included in this book. Unlike many other saints, there are no exhaustive written accounts of her life and most of the historians who refer to her at all say simply she was a virgin martyr who died for her faith, the victim of a heathen Saxon.

So, why is she here? Well, firstly, Lewinna is our only Sussex female saint. A native of this county, she was born in the 7th Century and as such is the oldest woman whose story we can tell. Secondly, the very fact that little is known about her is a mystery in itself For centuries after her death, her shrine was a centre of pilgrimage and miraculous healing, yet records of her were either not kept at all or were kept so carelessly that they were lost. Thirdly, however interesting the story of her life and death might have been, the story of her bones is not to be missed.

No one knows exactly when Lewinna was born or when she was martyred, but she is said to have been alive during the reign of Egbert who was king of Kent. She was still alive when Egbert died in 674 and outlived him by anything up to 15 years. Interestingly, although the exact year of her martyrdom isn't known, she is thought to have died on July 24th.

With great honour, she was laid to rest in a monastery dedicated to St. Andrew and there she remained undisturbed for three and a half centuries.

Lewinna's story might well have ended there. Although there has been plenty of speculation, no one knows just where the monastery was situated or even what kind of monastery it was. It could have been nothing but a small chapel or church. Whatever its structure, it has gone now and had it not been for an 11th century French monk named Balgerus, all trace of Lewinna might well have gone, too. Balgerus was a deeply religious ascetic from a Benedictine monastery at Bergues outside Dunkirk. He was also obsessed with saints and spent a good part of his time travelling in search of pieces of them to add to his monastery's collection. Sixteen years before he came across Lewinna, he made a point of getting to know Edward the Confessor in order to acquire relics of the English saints, Oswald and Idaberga.

The story of Balgerus and Lewinna is told by a monk called Drogo who wrote everything down on the instruction of the abbot at Bergues. The writing was long-winded and ungrammatical, but it's a true adventure story.

The tale begins in April 1058, with Balgerus preparing for yet another voyage to England in search of saintly bits and pieces. He booked passage on a merchant ship which was bound for our shores in the hope of selling its cargo.

All was going well until an unfavourable wind took hold, blowing them first towards Dover, then back out into the Channel where the ship was held for a day and a half As they approached the shore on the following day, the wind took hold again, buffeting the ship violently westward along the coast. They passed several ports, but were given no chance of entering the harbours and, in fear of their lives, the sailors began to pray.

Trying to calm his men, the captain said, "Not far from hence, I know for certain of two harbours which we may reach; if not the first, at any rate the second will be open to us by the help of God."

As the men continued to pray, they were carried within sight of the next port and quite suddenly, although the ship was still in full sail, they were swept safely through the narrow entrance.

Drogo calls the port Sevordt and goes on to give an accurate description of the mouth of the River Ouse which in those days joined the sea at Seaford. Exhausted, the crew slept.

When morning came again, Balgerus was eager to be off.

It just happened to be Easter Sunday and he wanted to celebrate the feast in a church. In the distance, he saw a spire and, taking a companion, set off towards it. The distance is given as three leagues. His actual destination remains a matter for conjecture. Records show there was a church dedicated to St. Andrew in Lewes and it has been said that the town took its name from Saint Lewinna or vice versa. Alfriston claims a monastery dedicated to St. Andrew, which is said to have stood on the site of the Parish church. Jevington, however, claims to have the only church spire visible from the point described in Balgerus' journey and the church there is also dedicated to St. Andrew.

Whatever his destination, when he was only half way there, Balgerus suddenly had to rest. A weakness and dread of mind had seized him. On feeling better, he started out again and almost immediately met an old man. Saintly relics never being far from his mind, Balgerus pointed to the spire and asked, "What monastery is that, what relics may be there, and to whose honour is it dedicated?"

"It is the Monastery of Saint Andrew which you see," the old man replied, "and the body of Saint Lewinna the virgin martyr rests there, whose merit is vouchsafed every day by heavenly power."

The old man asked if he wanted to know anything else, but the news of a saintly relic was enough for Balgerus and he was eager to be on his way.

The monk and his companion reached the monastery in time to attend mass and when the service was over, they made a careful examination of the church. On the wall, they found rolls of parchment covered in writing which they asked the priest to translate for them. He explained that they were lists of all the miracles which had been accomplished through the merits of Lewinna and told them that no matter how ill or infirm the pilgrims had been, every single one had been immediately cured.

Balgerus was inflamed by what he heard. He took the priest aside and offered him money. "Take whatever you want from me and give me a relic of this great virgin, a bone or some such, which I can take back to be honoured at my own monastery."

The priest was shocked and said as much in no uncertain terms. Balgerus blushed, pretended he'd only been joking and asked if he could stay and say masses. The priest agreed curtly and went about his business.

Left to his own devices, Balgerus began to chant and pray. He kept glancing sideways at Lewinna's tomb and occasionally stretched out a hand to stroke it as an ordinary pilgrim might. The temptation to steal her grew in his mind. The stroking became more searching until he accidentally discovered he could get into the tomb if he accidentally twisted the iron nails at one end and accidentally pulled them out.

The sight of Lewinna's bones wrapped in a red cloth seems to have touched Balgerus' conscience, because he quickly put the tomb back together again and got on with his prayers. It was only a brief niggle of his conscience, though, and he spent the whole of the following night praying for suggestions as to how he might carry Lewinna away.

The next morning, the man who was looking after the church wanted to go away for the day and innocently asked Balgerus if he would keep an eye on things.

"Go wherever you will, my friend, and I will guard everything as diligently as you would yourself," Balgerus lied happily.

Alone once more, he tried to lift the tomb, but to his horror it wouldn't move. He prayed for a while, then tried again. Again Lewinna wouldn't budge. Balgerus was stumped, but not for long. He put a leather strap round his neck and shoulders, attached it to the tomb, then called out, "Accept me, reverend virgin, as thy servant forever, only allow yourself to be moved and taken to where you will receive the veneration you deserve."

Balgerus heaved again and this time the tomb moved. Delighted, he asked Lewmnna, almost as an afterthought, that if his faithful theft was to go undetected, she should allow herself to be stolen. Of course, if he was going to be caught, he added, he would rather she stayed put.

He went back to singing the psalms and as he finished, he fell into a miraculous sleep during which Lewmnna appeared to him.

"Wake up," she said, "and take me with you as a companion on your journey."

Balgerus needed no second telling. He woke up, checked the church to make sure no one was watching and opened the tomb. Quickly, he began collecting Lewinna's bones in a piece of linen he had brought with him, but each time he tried to pick them up, a few small bones fell through a tear in the cloth. When it had happened three times, he realised Lewinna was telling him he should at least leave some part of her where she had ended her life. Doing as he was told, he gathered the rest of her together and carried her off to the inn where he was staying.

To allay suspicion, he sent his companion back to the ship with Lewmnna and remained at the inn. Another fierce wind blew up that night, but Lewinna appeared to Balgerus again and promised him fair weather in the morning.. The saint kept her promise, although the journey to Bergues wasn't all plain sailing. Balgerus was separated from the precious bones for a while, but eventually, he arrived back at the monastery to a great welcome.

Neither Balgerus nor Drogo appear to have seen anything wrong in kidnapping Lewinna's bones. They conveniently forgot about all the people who came to her shrine to be cured and assured themselves that Lewinna had been neglected and would be much better off in France.

While the monks stood by with torches, the saintly bones were washed in the best wine and placed in a gold and silver chest – which the local bishop firmly nailed down on every side to make sure no one else touched Lewinna with sticky fingers.

Presumably, she was happy in her new home, because Drogo goes on to list many cures resulting from her presence. Lewinna's bones stayed in Bergues until 1522 when most of them were destroyed during the religious troubles of the time. One piece of rib survived and was eventually placed in an elaborate silver reliquary and put on show again in the early part of this century. The 20th century, however, is an uncomfortable place for saints. During the last war, the whole of that part of Normandy was heavily bombed and the church at Bergues did not escape. The reliquary and the last fragment of Lewinna's physical presence disappeared – this time possibly for ever. ❑

LEE MILLER
(1907-1977)

"I LOOKED LIKE AN ANGEL, BUT I WAS A FIEND INSIDE."

L ee Miller is a difficult woman to categorise. You could say she was a fashion model, but she actually spent more time on the other side of the shutter and became a renowned photographer. You could call her a journalist, but that would miss the fact that she was also a war correspondent. She has been described as the beauty of her generation, a socialite and a surrealist and although she was probably all three, she was very much more. Imagining her in a peaceful Sussex village is equally difficult, yet that is where she lived in the latter part of her life. She was a woman who made normal life seem small, who inspired total devotion in her friends and lovers and drove everyone half crazy while she was about it.

She came from Poughkeepsie, New York, the only daughter of Theodore and Florence Miller. Her given name of Elizabeth was quickly shortened to Li Li and soon became Lee. With her two brothers, she enjoyed an idyllic early childhood on the small farm where they lived.

Theodore Miller was a gifted mechanical engineer and amateur photographer and he instilled in his children an inquisitiveness of mind and a fascination for science and adventure which never left them.

In 1914, when Lee was seven, her mother became ill for a short time and she was sent to friends in Brooklyn. The friends had a young son who was on leave from the United States Navy. No one knows exactly what happened while she was there, but when she returned home it was discovered she had been sexually molested and infected with venereal disease. Her mother had to administer the only cure available in those days, douching with dichloride of mercury – torture for both of them.

On the advice of a psychiatrist, to minimise any guilt she might later feel, Lee was taught that sex was merely a physical act which had nothing to do with love. It was a lesson which shaped many of her relationships throughout her life. Another traumatic event occurred when Lee was in her mid-teens. She had fallen in love for the first time. While she and her boy-friend were out rowing on a lake, he fell into the water, suffered heart failure and died instantaneously.

Lee's school days weren't easy, either. To try to compensate for the ordeals of her young life, her parents had indulged her at home. Lee had become manipulative and she didn't take kindly to discipline. A succession of schools failed to channel her spirit into what they considered an acceptable mould. Her quick brain was as curious as ever, but she was interested in her own curriculum, not her teachers' .

Relief came when Lee was offered a trip to France. She sailed to Europe, but far from being tamed by a more sober culture, as her parents had hoped, she instantly submerged herself in the intoxicating glamour of Paris and decided to become an artist. The surrealist movement had taken centre stage, hedonism had become the religion of the day and Lee was beautiful, gregarious and just 18 years old. For months her life whirled within circles influenced by people like Jean Cocteau, Gertrude Stein and Ernest Hemingway. In the end, her father had to go to Paris to fetch her home.

Back in Poughkeepsie, life seemed dull by comparison and Lee made trips to New York which lasted longer and longer. Always in search of excitement, she enrolled at the Art Students League and learnt to dance professionally, appearing briefly in the George White Scandals variety show and a night-club production called *The Great Temptation.* Then fate played a hand. Stepping carelessly in front of an oncoming car one day, she was pulled to safety by the magazine publisher, Condé Nast. Even as she collapsed into his arms, he must have been affected by her looks and her natural style. By March 1927, Lee was on the front cover of *Vogue.*

She was photographed by many of the most famous photographers of the day and she lived her new life to the full. Looking back in later life, Lee said, "I was terribly, terribly pretty. I looked like an angel, but I was a fiend inside."

Despite the excitement of running with the social and intellectual elite of New York, Lee became obsessed with returning to Paris. She secured a small commission from one of the fashion designers and an introduction to the American artist photographer, Man Ray, and sailed back to Europe. She had gained an interest in photography from her father, and she began using her amateur skill on her assignment, taking photographs of clothes in Renaissance paintings in Florence and sending them back to America.

By the time she arrived at Man Ray's studio in Paris, she had decided to become his pupil and she told him just that. He said he didn't take students and was leaving Paris for his holiday. Lee said, "I know, I'm going with you."

Lee lived with Man Ray for three years. It was a tempestuous affair and certainly not one which was mutually exclusive, but then Lee saw no reason why a sexual encounter with another man should affect the person she was in love with at the time. Meanwhile, she was becoming an accomplished photographer in her own right, learning to process her own work and to develop new photographic techniques. She took on assignments of her own for Vogue and other magazines and became a sought-after portrait photographer, and she was still modelling. A glass manufacturer designed a champagne glass inspired by the shape of her breast and she was said to have the most beautiful navel in Paris. In Jean Cocteau's film *Blood of a Poet,* she took the lead female role, playing an armless statue in the first scene. Later, describing the experience in Vogue, she began to display her talent for fresh, straightforward writing.

Lee met and became infatuated with an Egyptian named Aziz Eloui, a gentle, quiet man, nearly 20 years her senior. The feeling was mutual, but the complications in both their lives were more than Lee could stand and eventually, in November 1932, she left Paris, Man Ray and Aziz. She returned to New York and set up her own studio.

Almost immediately – a miracle, given the depression of the 30s – she became an established photographer working in portrait, fashion and commercial fields, experimenting with colour photography and strengthening links with *Vogue, Harper's Bazaar* and *Vanity Fair.* Then, Aziz arrived back in her life. In July, 1934, before anyone realised what was happening – possibly not even Lee herself – they were married.

Life in Cairo was obviously different from life in New York or Paris, but Lee entered into the social round with her usual boldness. She gambled, studied chemistry for six hours a week at the American

University and learnt Arabic. She travelled with Aziz to Saint Moritz, to London, to Jerusalem. It couldn't be said that she settled – Lee never settled to anything for long. Without work to stimulate her, she continually looked for outside diversion. She organised a group of friends, hired a guide and set off into the desert on a trip that was a near disaster. It wasn't until the guide had gone on ahead to scout the route that it was discovered Lee had filled the huge insulated water container with Martini cocktail. By the time the guide returned hours later, they were all suffering from dehydration aggravated by alcohol and almost raving with thirst.

It was the first of many journeys into the desert that lasted anything from a couple of days to several weeks. But even these organised adventures couldn't hold boredom at bay for long and in the summer of 1937, with Aziz's blessing and financial support, Lee returned to Paris. Within hours of her arrival, she was the centre of attention at a surrealist ball. She was introduced to Roland Penrose and by the time another 24 hours had passed, they had become lovers.

They spent a month together in Cornwall with the surrealist elite around them, debating, arguing and making love. A few weeks later they were in the South of France where Picasso was holding court. He painted Lee's portrait and Roland bought it for £50 and presented it to her. Aziz was overjoyed to see her when she finally went back to Cairo, but Lee was again unsettled. She resumed her desert journeys and indulged in other affairs, all the time keeping in contact with Roland. They met again in Athens in the spring of 1938, travelled together through Bulgaria and parted again at Bucharest.

When Lee again returned to Aziz, it was only really a token reunion and it was obvious their marriage was nearing its end. Roland actually visited Egypt and accompanied Lee on one of her desert journeys. In 1939, she sailed from Port Said and Aziz to join Roland in England.

The threat of war was in the air. They lived together, loved and travelled. When Hitler invaded Poland, they were in Antibes. Although Lee could have returned to America and safety, she chose the unknown adventure of war and returned to England with Roland.

The war years must have almost fulfilled Lee's need for excitement. She took up photography again, working for *Vogue,* at first on a succession of dull assignments, but gradually gaining greater recognition. Her creative talent flowered in the surrealist landscape of war-torn London. Her first story as a photojournalist was a thoughtful account of the experiences of American army nurses. Six weeks after D-Day, she was in Normandy. She saw tent hospitals and hitched a lift in a command car to a casualty clearing station within two miles of the front line. She took 35 rolls of film and returned to England to write one of the most impressive articles of her career. *Vogue* ran the story using 14 pictures in two double-page spreads. Lee was finally in her element. Soon she was back in France again on assignment for *Vogue*. The US Army Public Relations Office wanted her to cover a Civil Affairs team in Saint Malo as they helped re-establish civilian life after the fighting. Having hitched another ride, this time from Omaha Beach, she had arrived in the town to find the fighting still going on. Her descriptions of the air and ground attacks happening all around her captured the scene so well she made her readers smell the smoke. She photographed the effects of the new secret weapon, napalm, and sent them back to Vogue, but the British censor stepped in and banned them before the pictures could be published. Lee was still there, still taking photographs, when the German commander surrendered. Afterwards, she was put under house arrest in Rennes for entering a combat zone. She used the time to catch up on lost sleep and write the 10,000 word article of her experiences that Vogue published in October 1944. Free again, she entered Paris on the day of liberation. Shunning the political and military angles that other writers would use in their articles, she immediately began searching out her old friends – Picasso, the Eduards, Cocteau, Aragon and others – and scooped their stories. Then, even as the city began to breathe again, Lee was refocusing her cameras to capture Paris fashion.

Back at war, she covered the Alsace campaign, following the US forces as they struggled to cross the Rhine. She was in Torgau for the American link-up with the Russians on the banks of the Elbe. When Dachau concentration camp was liberated, Lee was one of the first people allowed through the gates. The terrible sights she saw there left her scarred for life. In a cold rage, she kept her camera clicking. Knowing many of her Jewish friends had perished in places like this, she wanted to confront the world with the atrocity of it all.

From Dachau, she went to Munich where she and Dave Scherman, the reporter she had been travelling and working with, were billeted in the captured German command post of the 45th Division at Prinzregentenplatz 27. The swastika and A. H. monogram on the silver was the only thing to show whose house it had been. Dave photographed Lee enjoying her first soak for weeks in Hitler's huge bathtub.

After the war was over, it took Lee a long time to come to terms with the overdose of adrenalin and excitement which had fuelled her days as a war correspondent. The war had changed her. If anything, it had made her even more unsettled and it affected her relationship with Roland. She spent time in Paris, Salzburg and Vienna reporting on Europe's return to so-called normality. From there, she went on to Budapest where she recorded everything from the social life of the city to the execution of Laszlo Bardossy, the former fascist Hungarian Prime Minister. Later, in a small village, she was taking photographs of an old woman working on her embroidery when she was arrested. This time it took a friend and a fake pass to secure her release. Although she had ignored Roland for months, they were soon reconciled when she finally returned to England. In the Spring of 1947, Lee was in Saint Moritz on assignment for *Vogue* when she discovered she was pregnant. After her return to England, Aziz came to visit her and with his usual generosity divorced her under Moslem law by reciting "I divorce thee" three times. Three days later, in July, Lee and Roland were married and in September, she gave birth to a healthy boy and named him Antony William Roland.

It was in early 1948 that she and Roland heard of the 120 acre farm at Muddles Green, near Hailsham. They went to see Farley Farm on a dreary February day and fell in love with the large square house and its views stretching ten miles to the South Downs and the Long Man of Wilmington. They purchased the property at auction only days later. Roland's involvement with London's art scene was keeping him extremely busy, but he had always enjoyed the idea of farming and he employed a manager to run the farm and a gardener. Lee took on a housekeeper cook and a nanny to look after Tony and entered into country life with the same gusto with which she did everything else.

She travelled with her husband in his work with the Institute of Contemporary Art and continued working on fashion features for *Vogue*, but she rapidly lost interest in peacetime journalism. Farley Farm became a meeting place for their enormous circle of friends and Lee loved entertaining. The guest list reads like a Who's Who of the art world – Picasso, Ernst, Eluard, Saul Steinberg, Henry Moore. Jean Dubuffet's arrival on the Newhaven ferry was just the coming of yet another eccentric. He couldn't speak English, but the taxi drivers at Newhaven were used to the goings-on at Farley Farm by then and delivered him unerringly to the door.

Bringing her usual eccentricity to the role of hostess, Lee expected all her visitors to make themselves useful sewing curtains, chopping wood, gardening, anything Lee could think of that needed doing. The last article she wrote for *Vogue*, published in 1953, was called, *Working Guests*, and featured a picture of Lee asleep on the sofa while her guests toiled around her.

The decision to stop writing was her own and it heralded the beginning of a traumatic period in Lee's life. She lost all interest in physical relationships, fought with Roland, drank too much, alienated her son. Luckily, her interest turned towards food, and cooking became the new challenge in her life. Surprisingly, she never wrote a cook book, but in the following years, she collected 2,000 cookery books and thousands more recipes. Now when she travelled with Roland, she would barge into hotel and restaurant kitchens and exchange recipes with the chefs.

In his book The Lives of Lee Miller, which forms the source material for this chapter, Antony Penrose has probably come closer than anyone to capturing his mother in a single sentence. He wrote: "A paradox of irascibility and effusive warmth, of powerful talent and hopeless incapability, Lee rode her own temperament through life as if she were clinging to the back of a runaway dragon."

Lee died of cancer at Farley Farm in 1977. She faced death without fear, as she had faced life. For her it was the start of a whole new adventure. ❑

NORTH END HOUSE HOME SCHOOL
(1882 – 1982)

THE LIFE WORK OF THE MISSES EDITH AND MARY DUMBRELL AND MISS HELEN KNOWLES

by Josephine Ferguson

In 1882, in a large farmhouse on the road leading out of Ditchling towards the Common, three sisters started a school which was to be utterly unique. It was a school with old-fashioned habits and customs, but which was none the worse for them. In fact, its quaint timeless quality and the high principles of the teaching staff, mostly women, made it a school that was much loved by the hundreds who passed through its doors during its century of existence.

The names of the three founding sisters were May, Edith and Mary Dumbrell. They started the school as a means of livelihood after the death of their father in a hunting accident on the Downs. Of May we know little, for she died young, but Miss Edith and Miss Mary (as they were always called by the pupils) continued to run the school with great success until their deaths – Miss Edith at 86 and Miss Mary at 91. Exemplary women, they always seemed to be able to bring the best out of their pupils. Although they ran the school as a business, they were far too kind to parents who couldn't pay the full fees so, even though they never became rich, they certainly enriched the lives of all the young people who came under their influence.

Originally the school was for boarders whose parents were in India or other parts of the Far East; the pupils could stay at the school during the holidays if necessary. Because of this the Dumbrells were good at teaching their pupils how to play and amuse themselves usefully as well as giving them an excellent academic grounding. Miss Edith had studied music in Germany and taught the piano; Miss Mary was qualified to teach English and was considered the 'brilliant one'.

The sisters taught their pupils to put other people first at all times, to have good manners and to be resourceful and ingenious. During the First World War, when there were no men to do the outside work, they set all the girls to work in lines cutting the grass in the hockey field with embroidery scissors. They used the same method to cut the grass on the graves in Ditchling Churchyard (this outing was always considered 'a treat'). The hard tennis court was marked with a toothbrush dipped in a bowl of white paint, and the circles on the netball court were drawn with a piece of string, a stick and a paintbrush.

Endurance was also taught – if a girl was untidy she was given a 'tidy mark', which involved lying flat on the bare floor for half an hour. Sometimes the whole floor was strewn with prone bodies.

There was no uniform. The only compulsory items were a Sussex sun-bonnet – even the mistresses wore them and they were made by Ada Cave in the village for three shillings (3/-) each – and a pair of gumboots, of which frequent use was made as each child had her own plot of garden. Botany was a speciality and there were numerous nature walks especially to spots where the rare Bird's Nest Orchid grew (in Nye Lane Woods), the Fly Orchid (in the same area) and the more common Bee Orchids on the Downs.

Many quaint rituals took place, such as the locking up of the sugar in a safe each night, by Miss Mary. This had started during the First World War and had continued ever since.

Despite food rationing during two wars, the meals at North End were renowned. There was always a choice between two meat dishes and two puddings, but it wasn't really a choice, as the girls knew that they had to 'go in turn' as it was called, otherwise there would not have been enough of one dish and too much of the other left over.

Miss Mary's sight was not too good for carving so she always had the shepherd's pie, rissoles or stew. Miss Edith took great care in carving the roasts. Armed with an array of carving knives, she would pick up one, then another, tut-tutting irritably because they were never sharp enough. The meat came from the two local butchers whose services the Misses Dumbrells would use alternately so as not to offend either one of them.

The puddings were dispensed as follows: suet ones by Miss Mary (treacle on Monday, baked bread on Tuesday, chocolate on Wednesday, jam on Thursday and ginger on Friday), whilst Miss Edith apportioned the stewed fruit or milk pudding.

When the Second World War began, the Dumbrells gave up taking boarders, as it was considered a dangerous area and, indeed, much of the Battle of Britain took place overhead. Later on, the school was well and truly in 'bomb alley', the route taken by bombers and doodlebugs heading in the direction of London.

Even though the school became a day school it did not lose its character. I attended the school from 1940 to 1947 and think with joy of sitting on a fallen tree-trunk, wearing a sun-bonnet and struggling with 'returned' algebra, looking towards an orchard in which soldiers were camped awaiting D-Day.

Miss Edith was tall and thin with a mass of white hair, swept upwards and pinned above her long, pale pink face. Known as the 'pretty one', she did look pretty when she smiled but she was so painfully shy she tended to look serious, and those who learned the piano were rather terrified of her.

Miss Mary was a complete contrast: much shorter and stouter, almost tubby like Pooh Bear; her hair always in an untidy bun above her round, humorous face. She was full of character and had such a grasp of politics and worldly things that, despite their sheltered life, she frequently scandalised Miss Edith by uttering extremely original and forthright remarks like: "Try and turn arguments into friendly discussions." These utterances were rendered more humorous by an unfortunate affliction which caused her to sound as if she had bad adenoids. She always said, for example, 'otherwizz' for otherwise. Her oft-repeated maxim was: "Don't do as I do – do as I say." Frequently, while reading to the class a passage that she considered to be amusing, she would stop, look up and say: "That was funny – will you all please laugh."

Miss Edith always dressed in blue and Miss Mary in grey. Their garments appeared to flow down to their ankles without anyone knowing the exact details of what they were wearing.'

Although not born in Sussex, Miss Helen Knowles lived here for 80 of her 90 years. She arrived at North End when she was ten and progressed to become head girl before leaving to do teacher training. When she was

24 she returned to teach and never left. She took over the school after the sisters died and named it Dumbrells in their memory. She increased the numbers in the school but only took pupils (including some boys) up to the age of 13 whereas the sisters had taken them to the age of 18.

Miss Knowles was a brilliant teacher – she could make the dimmest child understand when everyone else had given up on him or her, usually saying something funny which made them remember it forever. Such as the Lancashire cotton-spinning towns: "Oh, go and put your wig on and bury the old ham," she would shout in mock rage (Wigan, Bury and Oldham). Or reading, from *The Grammatical Kittens:*

"A preposition

Is a word that comes BEFORE a noun

TO the farmyard,

IN a basket,

Pussy came FROM Town."

She had a remarkable speaking voice and the children loved listening to her reading the classics. Even during the air raids, as the children squatted under their desks, she read to them from beneath her own. She uttered such maxims as : "Crying is only a means of feeling sorry for yourself' and "a lady is someone who doesn't mind what she does." This pronouncement was made after she had hung upside down, unblocking the frozen lavatories during the winter of 1947. She also milked the cows and was a great gardener. She often used to say that gardening taught patience: "A good gardener never hurries: he keeps at it from morning to night but never panics.

Some of the little ones feared Miss Knowles as they would an ogre, but her tongue was firmly in her cheek and as they grew older they realised this and were able to appreciate her sense of the ridiculous. Her humour helped to develop many a character.

A number of former pupils went on to achieve fame of one sort or another. Angela Goodenough was Chief Wren during the Second World War; Elizabeth Beresford of Womble fame was a day-girl for a short time and Camilla Shand attended before almost marrying Prince Charles.

One former pupil summed up the school when she said "it was like staying with kind aunts, who were also governesses – but they were not too kind." ❏

JOAN, LADY PELHAM
(c. 14th-i 5th century)
MIGHTY WITH PEN AND SWORD

The 14th century was a dark time in England. The people were troubled, conditions were often diabolical, thrones were unsafe and a third of the population of Europe perished because of the Black Death. It was a time when only the strong survived and even they needed their wits intact.

In this climate of hardship and disease lived a woman called Joan, Lady Pelham. Unfortunately the manorial records of her home, Pevensey Castle, were destroyed during the peasant uprising of 1381 and it is difficult to trace her parentage. She could have been the daughter of John Bramshott of Gatcombe on the Isle of Wight. She could also have been the daughter of Sir John Escures or even Herbert Vincent of Netherfield. The various accounts that do exist give the impression that the harder you search, the more fathers you will discover – much like Gundrada, another of our Sussex Women. All in all, considering the confusion of the reports which have been written over the centuries, it is ironical that Joan's great claim to fame is a letter. The end of the century loomed. Richard II saw many of his friends tried by the Merciless Parliament, then executed as traitors. He turned from the bravery he had shown in his youth when confronting the peasants in 1381, and became an embittered and tyrannical king. Henry Bolingbroke, the son of John of Gaunt, rose against the throne. Claiming he had come to recover his father's estates, he landed at Pevensey, then re-embarked and sailed to Yorkshire. Among his supporters was Sir John Pelham, Constable of Pevensey Castle.

The climax came in 1399. Sir John left Pevensey and joined Henry to prepare to do battle with the king. In his absence, supporters of Richard attacked and lay siege to Pevensey Castle where Joan had remained with a diminished garrison. Her situation was dire. For a while, she had no idea what had become of her husband; for all she knew, both he and Henry might already be lying dead on a battle field. Rallying her fighting men, she prepared to defend her castle and set Richard's supporters on their heels.

Against all odds, Joan was still bravely holding Pevensey when a letter came from Sir John in Pontefract. The relief of knowing her husband was alive, and might be in a position to help, inspired her to take up her own pen and write what became the first known letter to be written in English by a woman.

The spelling is strange to us and at some points may even be a misreading of old handwriting, but pronounced phonetically, the meaning of her words becomes clear. Despite the desperate circumstances, she begins in the style of the day with a long, unhurried greeting, then goes on to thank him for his letter:

"My dere Lord, I recommande me to your hie Lordeschipp wyth hert and body and all my pore mygth, and wyth all this I think zow, as my dere Lorde, derest and best yloved of all erthlyche Lordes: I say for me, and thanke yhow my dere Lord, with all thys that I say before, off your comfortable lettre, that ze send me from Pownefraite, that com to me on Mary Magdaleyn day: ffor by my trowth I was never so gladd as when I herd by your lettre, that ye warr stronge ynogh wyth the grace off God, for to kepe yow fro the malyce of your ennemys. And dere Lord iff it lyk to your hyee Lordescipp that als son als ye myght, that I myght her off your gracios spede, whyche God Allmyghty continue and encresse."

Joan had reached the midpoint of her letter here and it is only now that she comes to the point:

"And my dere Lord iff it lyk zow for to know off my ffare, I am here by layd in manner of a sege, wyth the counte of Susses, Sudray, and a grett parcyll off Kentte: so that lue may nogth out, nor none vitayles gette me, bot wt myche hard. Wharfore my dere iff it lyk zow,by the awyse off zowr wyse counsell, for to sett remedye off the salvation off yhower castell, and wtstand the malyce off ther schires foresayde. And also that ye be fullyche enformede of there grett malyce wyrkers in these schyres, whyche yt haffes so dispytffuly wrogth to zow, and to zowr castell, to yhowr men, and to zour tenaunts ffore this cuntree, have yai wastede for a grett whyle."

She ends: "Fare wele my dere Lorde, the Holy Trinyte zow kepe fro zowr ennemys, and son send me gud tythyngs off yhow. Ywryten at Pevensey in the castell on Saynt Jacobe day last past. By yhowr awnn pore J. Pelham".

At the time when Joan wrote this letter, the common written language among her class would have been French. It is possible that she had read Chaucer and she was obviously familiar with this style of writing – similar letters of approximately the same age written by men are in existence. The submissive style is, of course, deceptive. There was nothing submissive about Lady Pelham, as Richard's supporters soon found out.

She successfully defended the castle until Sir John could send reinforcements. Henry Bolingbroke captured Richard II, then claimed Richard had offered him the throne. He became Henry IV and rewarded the loyalty of Sir John Pelham and his wife with new titles and land. Sir John was also given the honour of bearing the royal sword on state occasions. But by then, Joan was already assured a place in our history books by her use of the pen as well as the sword. ❏

VERA G. PRAGNELL
(1896-1968)

STEERING STRAIGHT FOR THE HEART

At Longbury Hill, between Storringlon and Washington in West Sussex, lived a woman whose vision was of a different world from ours. She saw the darkness around her, the habitual struggle which life demands, and, unlike so many who give lip service to their ideals, she did something practical to make things better. She created a Sanctuary a place where people could escape from the stresses of their lives, where they could find shelter and peace, where no one was ever turned away.

Vera Pragnell was born in 1896, the daughter of a successful textile manufacturer, George Pragnell. After his death, she referred to him as a stimulus and a challenge. There is no doubt that she loved him dearly, but he was obviously a man who liked to lead from the front and, because she had relied on him totally, his death left her bereft. Unfortunately, she had also recently lost her only brother who had been killed in the First World

War and the double bereavement created an emptiness in her life which she was desperate to fill.

She spent some time studying sociology and economics which she called the most unsatisfying of sciences. The need to do some practical good in the world inspired her to join charitable and social organisations and under their guidance, she plunged herself into full-time work in the slums of London.

It was a frustrating experience. The trained, sincere workers like herself were so often hampered by those who seemed ignorant and sentimental. In her much gentler way, she had inherited her father's leadership qualities and she felt whatever good they achieved was only superficial – she always wanted to do more, to be more effective. She talked of a sinister and relentless force which was sucking men dry and she named it 'the industrial machine'. Man had lost the art of simple living through his own efforts.

She began to study psychology and simple country crafts and finally retreated to a tiny cottage at Haslemere on the borders of Sussex and Surrey where for a time she searched her soul in solitude.

The result of her search was the first Sanctuary.

The cottage door was thrown open to the world and inside was created a place of perfect peace. In the window, a light burnt constantly to welcome anyone who felt in need of food, shelter or the comfort of companionship. Vera described the Sanctuary as a personal and practical application of Christianity. Her vision didn't include an organised movement or a new cult – she wasn't interested in endless philosophical discussions which stimulated the brain, but did not feed the poor in body or spirit. She simply wanted to offer the possibility of a life which was actually worth the living.

Furnishings were mostly primitive and practical and the whole cottage reflected a monastic humility. There was no paid labour. Rates and taxes were paid with money gained from the sale of inessential possessions or items made by the people who came to find sanctuary. None of the residents had personal wealth to speak of – certainly not Vera – but if ever there was surplus money, it went to benefit the poor.

The first Sanctuary was a success, but it had its limitations. Given the space, the people who came would have been capable of supporting themselves, but the cottage was tiny and had little in the way of grounds. What they needed was land – and Vera began yet another search.

It took time, but eventually she discovered a pair of derelict semi-detached cottages at the foot of the South Downs on a tract of 19 acres of common and eight acres of arable land. The Haslemere cottage was disposed of and just before Christmas 1923, Vera gathered her few worldly goods together, packed them on her donkey and moved to Storrington.

As the cottages weren't habitable, she lived at first in a little caravan. The cottages were knocked into one and put into order and the land was divided into 12 half-acre allotments, pasture plots and sections where tents or shacks could be constructed to provide homes. A Belgian artist carved a cross which was erected on the heather covered hill within the Sanctuary grounds to serve as a reminder of the reason why the land had been made free. Again, no one was turned away and although this meant that many who came appreciated what Vera was trying to do, it also encouraged those who saw it just as a free home and meal ticket and who weren't even slightly interested in the philosophy behind it.

Vera didn't care. She gave without question to all who presented themselves at the door and trusted that if they weren't in contact with the spirit of the Sanctuary when they arrived, they would grow to understand. And if they never understood, she still didn't mind – to her they were still God's children. She wanted the Sanctuary to be a model which would inspire others like it to be built the length and breadth of Europe and beyond, until the whole world was a Sanctuary, where everyone worked for the common good, inspired by love for each other and for God. Perhaps if Vera had chosen a desert island for her Sanctuary, it might have been everything she wanted it to be. But she had chosen an ordinary piece of land in a community of ordinary people.

Locals, and some who were not so local, were quick with their criticisms and accusations. They accused Vera of encouraging free-love. She replied that she saw no harm in young people forging all kinds of beautiful friendships. They said she encouraged tramps. Tramps, she answered, were His people too. One newspaper called her a Lady Bountiful. Another said the Sanctuary was a hotbed of Communism. Vera said her critics were made up of the prudes, the humbugs and the dense – and she added, "Bless them!"

In 1927, she married the artist, Dennis Earle, and for several years they formed a united front against the outside world. But the continual controversy eventually took its toll and ten years after founding the Sanctuary, Vera fell ill. Her husband knew she needed to get right away and he took her to Tahiti to recuperate. While they were there, Douglas Fairbanks senior came to the island to film Robinson Crusoe and Dennis went to work for the film company designing sets.

When they returned to the Sanctuary 18 months later, it was in a poor state and Dennis took control and developed it into a more orthodox estate, building real houses to his own designs. One or two of the original settlers stayed, all the others drifted away, although Vera kept in touch with many of them. She and Dennis had a daughter, Deirdre, who eventually went to live in Ireland and Vera visited her when she could and enjoyed her five grandchildren.

When Vera died in 1968 at the age of 72, she was still living at the Sanctuary, still looking towards a better world. Her vision of life had been both supremely simple and perfectly practical. When lived successfully, she explained, such a lifestyle gave you a curious feeling – as if you had lived for countless years among echoes and were suddenly steering straight for the heart of the song. ❏

NANCY PRICE
(1880-1970)

NOBODY'S 'DARLING'

Nancy Price was considered a delicate child – an assumption she greatly resented as she grew older. In fairness to her parents, they did actually have grounds for their concern. Nancy suffered from asthma and bronchial problems for years and when she was still young, her father had to confiscate her violin because she practised so long that she began to develop a curvature. As far as Nancy was concerned, it was simply that her strength wasn't equal to everything she wanted to do and she found that extremely irksome. She wanted to fill life to bursting point – and in many ways, that is exactly what she did, becoming a distinguished actor, author and conservationist while living at her Sussex home in High Salvington near Worthing.

Nancy was born of Welsh-Irish stock, in Kinver, Worcestershire, in 1880. Her given name was Lilian and that is how she was known until she went on the stage.

She was a shy child, perhaps because she had few children of her own age to play with, and in many ways she grew into a shy adult. She adored animals, birds and insects and everything that kept her 'free from houses. From an early age, she kept a diary, filling it with impressions of the countryside around her, of rabbits at play, of walking over a pack-horse bridge, of the cry of a curlew. Frequently, her entries were pictorial, a sketch of waves breaking against the foot of a cliff, a painting of blue smoke drifting from whitewashed cottages. In later life she wondered if she might have done more with her art. Her obsession to become an actor began when she was 14, despite the fact that her father threatened to disown her if she took up such a disgraceful career. But she was quite determined and her golden hair, fair skin and obvious talent made sure she would catch a producer's eye. She made her first stage appearance at Birmingham when she was 19 having been given a non-speaking part as a member of F R Benson's company. Just five months later, she was on the London stage, playing one of the Pickers in *Henry V* at the Lyceum where she went on to play the role of Olivia in *Twelfth Night*.

She had a classic beauty which reflected her strength of personality and she modelled for a number of well-known artists and sculptors of the day, including Rodin. Recognition as an actor came with the part of Calypso in *Ulysses* which she played at His Majesty's Theatre in 1902. The role of Hilda Gunning in Pinero's *Letty*, which went on stage at the Duke of York in 1903, brought with it true success. She played literally hundreds of parts in her long career. Stage, television and film roles varied from Portia in *The Merchant of Venice* to the Rat-Wife in *Little Eyolf* from comedy to tragedy, but she is probably best known for her portrayal of Adeline, the hundred-year-old matriarch in Mazo de la Roche's Canadian family epic, *Whiteoaks*. The play opened in 1936 at London's Little Theatre and ran for two years, before moving to the Playhouse.

It was *Whiteoaks* that introduced Nancy to her parrot, Bonny. Nancy was holding a parrot audition at the Playhouse for the part in *Whiteoaks* and had seen 127 birds of all sizes and colours when Bonny was brought in. She was in a small box with a wire lid. Her plumage was in poor condition and her temper was worse – she had to be handled with padded gloves to begin with, but Nancy was immediately drawn to her and they became constant companions. In her time, Bonny became almost as famous as Nancy, appearing in 1,327 performances and never missing a cue.

Nancy wrote five books on birds, the last of which was published when she was 79. Her uncluttered, honest style describes Bonny's many exploits as if they were everyday events – walking along the pavement behind Nancy on the way to the London theatre, shopping together in

Worthing, being rescued from the top branch of a tree by the fire brigade, sitting unperturbed during the war while the big guns were being tested on the Downs not far from their cottage.

In a Registry Office wedding, Nancy married another actor, Charles Maude. He came from a large family which, initially, the shy Nancy found daunting. As a Colonel during the war, he was awarded the DSO and she described him as 'a gallant gentleman and a brave soldier'. Sadly, he died in 1943, but he left Nancy with two daughters, Elizabeth and Joan.

In her lifetime, she came to know many famous people.

As a child, she had met Queen Victoria, quite without realising who she was. She had accompanied her father to Cowes where he indulged his love of sailing every year. Occasionally, he would let Nancy go on the water with him, but she spent most of her time exploring the countryside on her tricycle. One day she saw a pony-carriage carrying a large man and an old lady. She watched as they stopped in a field, unpacked a hamper, a table and a chair and proceeded to eat a picnic. Naturally, Nancy's devotion to animals took her over to the pony. The old lady saw her and asked if she was hungry. When she said she was, the lady invited her to join them. Although Nancy was never permitted to suck chicken bones at home, she allowed herself the treat this time because the old lady was busily sucking hers. In church at Whippingham on the following Sunday, she saw the old lady again and asked her father if he knew who she was. "That," he said , "is the Queen of England."

Nancy saw her twice more. Once at Victoria's Diamond Jubilee and again at the old Queen's funeral.

She worked with most of the great actors of the day, ate an omelette cooked by Aiphonso XIII, entertained George V and Queen Mary in her green-room and met the Emperor of Abyssinia in a railway carriage. She knew several Prime Ministers and was struck by how dissimilar they were.

"I was completely at ease with Baldwin," she once said, "never quite so at ease with Neville Chamberlain or Asquith; intrigued by Ramsay MacDonald, provocatively roused by Lloyd George, affected by the integrity of Attlee, inspired by Churchill."

Nancy was 'green' long before the word was coined to describe conservationists and environmental issues. She was associated with the Ashington Sanctuary for Sick and Injured Birds and she battled successfully to save an area of Downland at Honeysuckle Lane from industrial development. In Beach House Park in Worthing, she erected a monument to the 'Warrior' homing-pigeons which were lost in both world wars.

She described herself as a person who didn't suffer fools gladly. Although she had an affinity for ordinary working people, she was irritated by the pretentious. She disliked parties and, unlike many of her profession, refused to call everyone 'Darling' . She felt it was degrading to be expected to take people out to lunch in order to get work and she only did so once. The man she was trying to impress was a theatre manager. He chose Claridge's and Nancy had to pawn the only valuable ring she possessed to pay for the meal. She landed the contract, but she said later that somehow she felt terribly ashamed.

When George VI awarded her the CBE in 1950, she received 4,000 letters and telegrams of congratulations. She loved her work and most of all she loved her writing, because, she said, it combined fearful responsibilities, adventurous opportunities and the thrill of creation. Her greatest delight and happiness came through her love of animals, birds and all nature. She said that when she died, she wanted to be laid in the earth with an acorn in her hand, so that her body would give something of service back to the land which of necessity it had so constantly raped in life.

When she did die at the age of 90 in 1970, her body was cremated at Worthing Crematorium, but although she didn't leave behind an oak tree in quite the way she wanted, in her books about her experiences and her animals, she left something of even greater worth – the memories of a life which had entertained many thousands and which can still be an inspiration. ❏

MISS MABEL RAYMONDE-HAWKINS, MBE
(1902-1998)

RAYSTEDE CENTRE FOR ANIMAL WELFARE
by Amanda Wilkins

"I have decided to use my home and gardens and the remainder of my life on behalf of needy animals," pronounced Miss Mabel Raymonde-Hawkins in 1950.

So began the Raystede Centre for Animal Welfare in Ringmer, near Lewes – where she took a very active part in the running of the centre for nearly half a century.

Born in Reading in Berkshire on April 7th 1902, Mabel was an only child. Her father died when she was five years old so her formative years were mostly influenced by her mother and maternal grandfather. She came from a long line of teachers and preachers, and, after graduating from Reading University, she followed the family tradition and moved to her adopted county when she took up a teaching post in a primary school in Worthing in 1929.

During the years leading up to the Second World War, she was a supply teacher and worked for brief or longer spells in 104 schools in the county whenever illness or other reasons meant a teaching position was vacant. But her peripatetic life ended with the war years – she was the headmistress of Fairwarp primary, to which had been evacuated a large London school.

She gave up teaching at the end of the war and went to work for a number of the bigger animal charities. But she did not stay with any of them for long as she felt that not enough of the public's money was benefiting the animals – there were just too many overheads and too much extravagance.

In 1950, she decided to branch out on her own and made a promise to herself that she would 'never say no to the needy animal.' So, with her companion Mrs Lipley, she founded her own charity and this was officialy registered in 1952. Every penny they received went to the animals and the two took nothing out for themselves.

When Raystede started it was just two and a half acres. "I remember buying the first row of stables, the first typewriter and choosing the first van which became an ambulance," recalled Miss Raymonde-Hawkins. "The money that came in for the first seven years was far short of our needs and so Mrs Lipley and I remained completely voluntary, putting our time into it and taking nothing out."

This explains why the centre had such a good foundation – the needs of the animals were put first. "Too many places do not stress the word welfare," she added.

Surprisingly, Miss Raymonde-Hawkins did not call herself an animal lover. Although she was brought up with a spaniel and had a pony when she was young, she said she was not stupidly fond of animals. "I want justice for animals. This century has been the worst because it has not attempted to stop zoos and circuses. It has given publicity to the sorrows and experimentation in laboratories, but it has not stressed the virtues of alternative medicines." The centre's vet has studied homeopathy and the ultimate aim is that all animals who arrive at Raystede in need of treatment are treated using only natural methods and products.

Miss Raymonde-Hawklns was a living example of the benefits of homeopathy. "I've never had any orthodox medical treatment; never taken any drugs, not even an aspirin, and at my age I'm not likely to start," she said proudly. She put her fitness down to not eating too much.

But she had been ill – twice. She suffered a very bad bout of influenza at the end of the First World War and in 1986 she had a period of being 'off the air' for about a month. She was, in fact, in a coma for ten days following a coronary.

Also she had never eaten meat. "I don't call myself a vegetarian. I was brought up as a non meat-eater – both my parents didn't eat meat. If no one ate meat the animals would not have to be loaded and off-loaded, and prodded on their way to the slaughter house."

She was firmly of the opinion that all nature is one and there is a rhythm of life which runs through it. She said everybody has 'natural intuition' – for her it was what kept her young and which sparked off her tremendous enthusiasm which rubbed off on all her staff at Raystede. "I would hate to work for me," she admitted wryly. "I know how high my standards are, so it must be very difficult."

But her supporters, known as the Friends of Raystede, appreciate these high standards. The Friends numbered more than 8,000 and she kept in touch with them through the Centre's quarterly magazine. By appealing to them for help, she managed to build Raystede into what it is today.

Adjacent fields have been bought by supporters each buying one square metre until the whole money was raised. Raystede now has 49 acres. Over the years, literally thousands of animals from terrapins and turtles, to donkeys and dogs, rats and rabbits – have all found a safe and caring home in the immaculately kept cages and runs.

"It annoys me that so many people call themselves animal lovers when they really want the animals as possessions, like dogs to guard them," she said. "My own dog is a wonderful guard but I would never have a dog solely to guard me. My responsibility in life is for me to equally guard that dog and all other life that is here."

She had no regrets about her single status. "I haven't had time to consider it," she said. "I've run Raystede on very thrifty lines, although no one knows what thrifty means these days. Children today have too much pocket money and they are not trained in courtesy and thought for others. We have always put the animals first and we have no one here who is overpaid – but we believe 'the labourer is worthy of his hire'."

Miss Raymonde-Hawkins did not confine her animal welfare work to Sussex. She persuaded the Venice authorities to pay for 800 spay and neuter operations a year to control the large cat population in the Italian city. In Ireland, she was instrumental in buying a farm so that mares owned by gypsies could have their foals there rather than by the roadside. As part of this programme a vet is paid to visit the gypsy camps and treat their animals. Achievements such as these meant more to her than the

MBE she was awarded in 1975 by another nonagenarian, the Queen Mother.

"I shall only stop working when Jesus decides it is time for me to have a rest. Mind you He is taking a long time to decide whether He wants me or not," she added towards the end of her life. Raystede's work will live on into the 21st century thanks to Miss Raymonde-Hawkins' hard work in the latter half of the 20th century. ❑

Since the first edition of this book was published in 1995, Miss Raymonde-Hawkins died on January 17th 1998.

CHARLOTTE SMITH
(1749-1806)

THE PEARL THAT HAD BEEN BASELY THROWN AWAY
by Tamara Babadi

It is every aspiring writer's wish to be published. To reach this heady pinnacle with a first novel and make enough money to live on, however, is for the majority of writers an unattainable dream. Yet, before Jeffrey Archer set pen to paper and wrote his way out of penury, there was another writer who broke through the barriers of conformity and whose work became the forerunner of the modern novel: Charlotte Smith.

Her name does not automatically spring to mind when discussing great novelists and poets of the 18th century, yet Wordsworth said of her: "English verse is under greater obligations than are likely to be either acknowledged or remembered." How right he was, for Charlotte Smith was as popular in her day as Trollope was in his, even though her name has been lost in the mists of literary time.

But what were the circumstances that led this gentlewoman to write so prolifically over the 57 years of her life?

Charlotte was the eldest daughter of Anna Towers and Nicholas Turner. She was born in St. James', London, on May 4th 1749, into the world of the landed gentry. When she was three, her mother died bearing a son, and Charlotte and her siblings were sent to Nicholas' country seat at Stoke-next-Guildford to be cared for by their mother's sister.

Charlotte's aunt disapproved of 'Bluestockings' and set about instilling in Charlotte the graces suitable for society. Her aim was to provide her niece with the necessary skills to attract a wealthy husband. Charlotte was sent to an elementary school in Chichester and by the time she was eight years old, she was entered into a Kensington finishing school.

Charlotte's extraordinary talents came to light very early on. Her water-colours showed a mature understanding of technique and conception. By the time she was ten, she could draw, dance and speak French. Yet her love of reading and her composition of poetry met with her aunt's disapproval. When she illicitly subscribed to a circulating library, it was only her father's quiet encouragement that gave Charlotte access to good reading matter. Academically forward, she gained no satisfaction from the trivial romances which were provided for young ladies at the time, but found pleasure in the classics which were to be the foundation of her later writing.

When Charlotte was ten, her father bought Bignor Park, near Pulborough in Sussex, and it was there that Charlotte found a permanent source of inspiration for her writing. Scattered throughout her novels and poems are countless references to the influence of the Sussex landscape. This keenly felt sonnet, *To the South Downs,* is just one example:

'Ah! hills belov'd – where once a happy child,
Your beechen shades, "your turf, your flowers among",
I wove your bluebells into garlands wild,
And woke your echoes with my artless song,
Ah! hills belov'd – your turf, your flowers remain;
But can they peace to this sad breast restore;
For one poor moment soothe the sense of pain,
And teach a breaking heart to throb no more?
And you, Aruna? – in the vale below,
As to the sea your limpid waves you bear,
Can you on kind Lethean cup bestow,
To drink a long oblivion to my care?
Ah no! – when all, e'en Hope's last ray is gone,
There's no oblivion – but in death alone!'

Charlotte was 15 when she married Benjamin Smith. It was not a love-match, more a marriage of convenience – her father wished to marry a wealthy woman who could bring financial stability to his life and he knew the spirited Charlotte would not accept a stepmother.

Benjamin Smith was the second son of Richard Smith, a director of the East India Company. He was wealthy, but moved in less refined circles than Charlotte and when they took up residence above his father's shop in London, she soon realised her mother-in-law did not approve of her or her cultural interests. The harassment only ceased when her mother-in-law died, but Charlotte had become depressed by the knowledge that she had nothing in common with the people around her. She longed for the tranquillity of Bignor Park where she would not be thought strange.

The widowed Richard Smith was fond of her and would not have approved the behaviour of his son had Charlotte confided in him. She had realised very early on in her marriage that Benjamin was a wastrel whose ways would lead them to financial ruin, and she did her best to hide his extravagances from his father.

Her first child died within days of the birth of her second, and because Richard Smith was concerned about Charlotte's health, he moved the family to Southgate. Charlotte was alone for the first time since her marriage and she confided to her sister, Catherine Anne, that she regarded herself as 'a pearl that had been basely thrown away'. Her children and her books were her only solace. This was to be the first of many moves. At one point, when Richard was accused of libel, he looked to Charlotte for help. She defended him successfully and he attempted to persuade her to move to the city and become an assistant in his business. Although grateful, she yearned for the freedom of the countryside and persuaded her father-in-law to set Benjamin up as a gentleman farmer at Lys farm in Hampshire. They lived there for nine years and, by the time Charlotte was 25, she had borne nine children.

It was while they were in Hampshire that Richard Smith died. Her father-in-law's will had been drawn up with the intention of ensuring his grandchildren equal legacies. Charlotte was one of the executors, but the main responsibility for executing the will was Benjamin's and he was unfit for the task. Richard's will, although well-meaning, was elaborately worded and Charlotte spent the rest of her life fighting for her children's right to inherit. The bitter struggle and the hatred she came to feel for the legal profession emerges repeatedly in the mocking characterisation of her novels.

Benjamin Smith played the squire and gave full force to his hair-brained schemes for making money. Charlotte satirised him in her first novel, Emmeline, but she was soon to prove that she was a loyal wife who was willing to stand by the husband she neither loved nor respected. When Benjamin was thrown into the King's Bench prison for debtors, Charlotte handed over her children to her brother's care and stayed for most of the time in prison with her husband. During ,this self-imposed imprisonment, Charlotte witnessed two attempted break-outs and became schooled in the complexity of the law and of its manipulation by the rich and powerful.

It was while Benjamin was in prison that Charlotte decided to publish the poetry she had been writing since her childhood. Unperturbed by the first rejection, she sought assistance from her Sussex neighbour, the poet, William Hayley. Through his recommendation, and at Charlotte's expense, the poems were published by Dodsley. Her confidence was justified. Within a year of the publication of her Elegiac Sonnets, 1784, a second edition was called for – it was the first of many and gave Charlotte the initial indication of success.

Three months after Benjamin was released from prison, he was in trouble again and had to leave the country. They sailed to Dieppe and spent the winter of 1785 in a mouldering chateau. It was there that Charlotte gave birth to another son. She also found the time to translate Manon Lescaut, which she published on her return to England in the spring of 1786. She withdrew it when she was criticised for translating an immoral work and in 1787 published instead *The Romance of Real Life*, which was a translation of several different stories.

The family moved to Woolbeding in Sussex and Charlotte, beset with financial troubles and the complications of her father-in-law's will – as well as her husband's extravagances – resolved to support herself and her children by writing. From that day on, it was a determined fight to achieve some kind of security for her family, and the constant work that this entailed helped to embitter her. The social conventions and injustices of her time were attacked in a series of outspoken and satirical works. Indeed, her violent denunciation of inherited wealth and property would meet with the approval of the modem socialist.

In *The Old Manor House,* her finest character creation, Grace Rayland, is jealously proud that the Raylands did not lower themselves by marrying into the trading classes and Charlotte draws her with satirical perfection. Sir Walter Scott considered Grace Rayland as 'without a rival; a Queen Elizabeth in private life, jealous of her immediate dignities and possessions, and still more jealous in the power of bequeathing them'.

After finally leaving Benjamin in 1787, Charlotte decided she would write with one motive only – to be financially independent. It took eight months to write her first novel, and the four volume, *Emmeline*, or, *The*

Orphan of the Castle, was published in 1788. It was an instant success and soon went into a second edition.

In eight years she was to write 32 volumes of novels as well as children's books. She succeeded in maintaining herself and her family in the station in life to which she had been born. Her prolific ability to write easy, natural prose, to compose quickly and to draw on a rich set of experiences, gave her novels a character unique in the literary world of the 18th century.

But personal success hardly alleviated her growing ill-health and the continued family tragedy. Her third son, Charles Dyer, had his leg amputated after the siege of Dunkirk in 1793 and was to die of yellow fever while sorting out his grandfather's bequests in the West Indies in 1801. Her favourite daughter, Anna Augusta, died in 1794. Charlotte's publisher blamed her publicly for the delay in publishing *The Wanderings of Warwick* in 1794, disregarding the fact that by then her hands were crippled with arthritis.

The last years of her life were spent in restless wandering. She lived in Brighton, London, Oxford, Weymouth, Exmouth and Bath. In *The Wanderings of Warwick,* she wrote of how 'the unhappy almost always fancy that a change of place will relieve them' .

Charlotte died at Tilford, near Farnham, in 1806, six months before the final legal settlement of her father-in-law's will. She had survived her husband by a few months and was herself survived by eight of her 12 children. Charlotte Smith was not a great writer, but she was a distinguished one, and English literature and succeeding generations of novelists owe her a considerable debt. She brought a new significance to natural description in her narrative, using nature to create mood – unlike her contemporaries who gave merely description. But her greatest contribution, and the one that would become the template for the modern novel, was her use of characterisation. She introduced a realism to her characters that had never been exploited so thoroughly before and brought to fiction a new kind of heroine – an intellectual. She analysed the mental state of these women, used natural dialect and idiosyncratic speech, and, it could be said, anticipated the realistic novel and the psychological novel of today. In her methods, her manners and her opinions, she was a woman born before her time – a modern woman, tied to the stifling conventions of the 18th century. ❑

SUSANNAH STACEY
(1812-1893)

HOSPITABLE HERBALIST AND HEALER
by Elsie Anderson

When Susannah Hooker ran away from home just before her 20th birthday, her parents must have suffered a great shock. This beautiful, vivacious young woman from a wealthy home had a very privileged lifestyle. She rode regularly to hounds with her brother, and her reputation of being a fearless rider brought her many admirers. She was also very practical – her mother, who knew a great deal about herbs and their medical properties, passed this knowledge on to Susannah when she was just a little girl. She also taught her to be an excellent housekeeper. Many an upper-class family would have welcomed Susannah into their home as a daughter-in-law, but she turned her back on all her suitors and secretly married William Stacey

Helped in her conspiracy by a cousin, she hired a coach and the two of them drove to Cuckfield Church for the ceremony. It was surprising that

113

out of all her admirers she chose to marry William, for not only was he a farmer and several years her senior – but he was a widower with five children.

William's home was Stantons Farm in the . tiny village of East Chiltington, near Lewes. Susannah must have had a strong character to have coped with her new situation. Married to an older man probably set in his ways, and becoming overnight a step-mother to his four sons and daughter could not have been easy. However, she soon settled into her role as mistress of the house. After reorganising her new home and ready-made family to her liking, she set about taking charge of the farm. She began with the dairy and got that working to her liking and then she turned her attention to the hens and the hen houses. Finally, when the supply of eggs was to her satisfaction, she planted out her herb garden.

She was a strict disciplinarian, but she was also very fair and her step-children and staff adored her. Compared to many servants in Victorian times, her employees enjoyed a decent standard of living. In return for a good day's work, they were paid, as well as housed and fed. The kitchen maids received instruction in the making of sausages and cheeses, pickling pork, smoking hams and mixing the flakiest of pastry for the many pies that were made. They also learned how to make candles, soap and polishes. The brewing of beers and the making of wines and liqueurs at Stantons often required the assistance of neighbours to help with the bottling. A year later they would willingly return for the sampling.

Stantons became legendary for its hospitality. The wonderful food and fine wine that always seemed to be available, brought visitors from all over the county. Lord Sheffield was a frequent caller accompanied by any guest he might have staying with him at Sheffield Park. Once Garibaldi visited and to mark the occasion Susannah concocted a new liqueur that she named after him. Made from gin, sloes and bitter almonds, it was plum coloured to match his coat.

William and his sons were keen country sportsmen and by tradition the Southdown Hunt always held its first meet of the year at Stantons. On these occasions, Susannah served an enormous breakfast to the riders, their wives, children, grooms and servants. Her special stirrup cup, known as lumping powder', sent the Master and the huntsmen after the fox in high spirits. All who drank this concoction declared that after just half a glass they could get their horse to jump the highest hedges and the widest streams.

On their return after the hunt they would find Susannah's table laden with delicious pies and puddings, and liberal supplies of wines and beers to wash them down. 'Devil's Driver' was another favourite drink – served on leaving, it kept the men safe from evil on their way home.

Nothing was ever wasted at Stantons. Substantial meals were made from any leftovers to give to the poor who arrived daily at the door which was always open. Amongst other delights the desperately hungry could enjoy a good broth made from fish heads, fins and bones flavoured with onion, or bread and dripping, then a pudding of rice, sugar and milk, or a sago pudding. Invariably, when these poor people left Stantons, it was with a full stomach, warm clothing and their aches and pains relieved. Susannah was particularly strict about her medicine bottles – these were never to be lost or sold, but washed and returned to the farm.

Once her herb garden was under way, Susannah produced a whole range of products, not just medicines and poultices but perfume, skin cream and shampoo. She had the gift of healing; with this and the expert knowledge of herbal remedies she cured many of the patients who regularly came to the farm seeking help. She would prescribe drinking camomile tea for digestive problems, or thyme tea for a good tonic. Borage leaves used in a salad or put into wine were supposed to relieve melancholy.

Susannah used all manner of flowers, plants and herbs. Marigolds, a versatile ingredient, were used in wine, puddings, pickles and cheese, or distilled in water to take the pain from red or watery eyes. The dried leaves of marjoram soaked in boiling water and made into a poultice gave wonderful relief to rheumatism sufferers. She healed festering wounds with a concoction of Madonna lily petals sterilised in brandy. Every herb in her garden had several uses. Apart from their curative properties, they flavoured food, kept rooms sweet smelling, or aided teeth cleaning and hair washing. Susannah made hair lotion specially for the men in her family, which they rubbed frequently into their scalps – none of them ever went bald. Rosemary, thyme and cloves crushed together and placed in a drawer or wardrobe was an effective moth repellent.

The local doctor became a close friend and often carried her remedies in his black bag. He would tell his country patients to go and see Mrs Stacey first before he rode out to visit them from Lewes. He and Susannah would sit and discuss medical matters for hours on end, and one day the doctor persuaded her to experiment with the belladonna plant. (Although highly poisonous, alkaloid derivatives from the plant were used in sedatives, stimulants and antispasmodic drugs). This she did and the purity of the essence she obtained was acclaimed by doctors far and wide.

Greatly encouraged, she decided to grow belladonna on a large scale. The chalky soil of the South Downs was perfect for growing the plant and Susannah soon established a plantation. Every year, with the help of her sons, she kept the crop coming. The plantation only fell into disuse when manufacturers in Germany and Austria began producing the essence in much greater quantities.

However, during the First World War, long after Susannah's death, stocks of belladonna became scarce. A chemist asked one of Susannah's sons if he knew of anywhere locally suitable for growing the plant. The son returned to the plantation that his step-mother had planted 50 years earlier and found the belladonna flourishing profusely in the wild. The area was redeveloped and soon yielded a good supply. The demand ceased after the war, but traces of the plant are still on the Downs.

Susannah also worked her healing powers on animals. It is even recorded that she managed with her potions and charms to bring under control an outbreak of the dreaded foot-and-mouth disease.

As she grew older, Susannah became known to all as Grandma. With her potions, faith healing and supernatural powers some thought of her as a witch. However, she declared herself a devout Christian and never failed to attend the lovely Norman church just down the lane from the farm every Sunday. At Stantons, Sundays were always kept as a special day and only the most necessary work was done.

One February day in 1893, when Grandma was 81, she sent for a lawyer and, with much family apprehension, she made her will. Then to fulfil her own prophecy that she would die ten years after William, she took to her bed. She summoned one of her sons to ride to Lewes and fetch her great friend, the doctor. He came at once and spent a long time alone with her and when he left he looked very grave. She then asked for her youngest and favourite son to come to her. To him she imparted all her knowledge of faith-healing, the use of charms, and recipes of herbal remedies. She also told him the secret of how to put a curse on an enemy.

The next day, according to her instructions, her personal maid dressed her in a linen robe, her best lace cap, white stockings and shoes and a white velvet gown. Thus attired, she lay all day on her flower-strewn bed.

When the news got around the neighbourhood that Grandma was preparing to die, people from all over the parish began arriving at the farm. To avoid her being disturbed by the noise of carriage wheels and horses' hooves, her family had straw laid on the driveway. The many friends, both rich and poor, that she had helped so much, filed quietly past saying their last farewells. All were aware they were losing a very special friend.

When everyone had gone, Grandma closed her eyes and, without any fuss, passed away. Her grave is next to her husband's in the peaceful little churchyard at Westmeston, overlooked by her beloved South Downs. A wise and much-loved woman of Sussex, who used her wonderful gifts to give help wherever and whenever it was needed.❏

116

MRS STEERE AND MISS PICKMAN
(c. 19th century)
GRAVE DIGGERS OF LEWES

No disrespect is meant to Mrs Steere or to Miss Rickman for linking their names in this book because both are women worthy of note and they do have an interesting connection – they were't both concerned with graves.

It's possible they didn't even know each other, although they might well have done – they both lived in Lewes in the same part of the 19th century and despite the fact that very little is known about them now, they weren't the kind of women whose activities allowed them to go unnoticed in their day.

Mrs Steere was the wife of the sexton at All Saint's and Cliffe cemetery. She was one of those people who seem always to have been old. Her hands were gnarled, her body bent and her face was stained by her habit of taking snuff Her black skirt and flannelette blouse were said to hang on her body like sacks and her old black bonnet was often askew.

Despite her appearance, she was a determined woman and physically strong despite her years. When her husband died, she took up his spade and carried on his work digging graves.

Although she was a woman of great humour, who enjoyed listening to a joke as much as she enjoyed telling one, she took her work as a grave digger very seriously. It was said she prepared her charges' last resting places with the care of a mother preparing her baby's first bed.

She lived in a cottage beside the graveyard and was feared by the children who liked to play among the gravestones, Mrs Steere's voice would rise: "Get off there – don't you know where you be?" and send them creeping away. But at other times, if they treated the graves with the respect Mrs Steere thought was their due, she would charm the children into becoming her friends and talk to them of the flowers and animals that made her graveyard beautiful. She died around 1900 and was laid in her own carefully prepared burial place. Towards the end of her life, she could no longer dig the graves herself, but although her eyes were failing, she was always on hand to make sure the new grave diggers did their job properly.

Miss Rickman treated her graveyards with just such reverence, though her graves were of a different kind. A Quaker by faith, she kept an austere routine, getting up at four every morning and going to bed at four every afternoon, but although she was strict with herself, she was a kind woman who had a soft heart.

On her way home one day, she was shocked by the sight of a wagoner beating his horse. The creature was completely exhausted and had fallen in the shafts and no matter what its owner did, it couldn't find the strength to rise. Miss Rickman was a great lover of horses. She immediately offered the wagoner a good price for the animal and took it home to her stables where she brought it back to health and kept it in comfort for the rest of its life.

When the horse died, she arranged for it to be buried in the field next to her house and held a funeral at 6 am., making sure all the workmen who had dug the grave were there. An iron fence, painted bronze and picked out in gold-leaf, was set up around the site and the workmen all received half a sovereign for their trouble.

In time, Miss Rickman buried three more horses, the last of which was her own beloved steed, Charlie. For him she had a great mound built with a centre of solid concrete. On the summit she laid a granite stone inscribed with lead lettering and, climbing up to it, she made a spiral path bounded by a hedge and fence. Until her health failed, every day at noon she made a pilgrimage to the very top. ❏

SUSANNA SWAPPER AND ANN TAYLOR
(c.17th century)
RYE'S WITCHES

Sussex has always been a good county for witches. Throughout Europe, there have been whole centuries when a woman couldn't look at someone sideways for fear of causing offence and risking the ducking stool, or worse, the rope or the fire. Presumably, Sussex has had just as many witches as anywhere else, but for some reason, they have been less likely to be called to justice. In the 150 years leading up to the beginning of the 18th century, almost a 100 people were brought before the Assizes charged with witchcraft in Kent; in Essex the total reached almost 300. For the same period. Sussex managed just 18, an average of about one witch every eight years.

Of course, people were charged with witchcraft in other types of court, but even then, Sussex seemed particularly easy going where broomsticks and pointed hats were concerned.

119

It is an unusual story then, that brought two women to trial at the same time. The case of Mrs Ann Taylor and Mrs Susanna Swapper was held in Rye in 1607 and a very peculiar one it was. The women's families were actually next door neighbours, living in Lion Street at the time. Susanna was brought before the Mayor for questioning and her story went like this.

One night, around midnight, when she was lying in bed, four ghosts appeared – two men, one young and one old, and two women. They didn't seem particularly interested in frightening her and the young man actually introduced himself as Richard. Next day, Susanna told Ann what had happened, but her friend wasn't impressed and accused her of imagining things. The ghosts appeared twice more and when Susanna next said something about her nocturnal visitors, Ann took more notice. Being a pragmatic woman, she suggested Susanna ask them what they wanted. The ghosts obligingly appeared again and when the question was put to them they said Susanna should fetch Ann into the garden and tell her to start digging. Into the garden Ann came and both women began to dig in great excitement thinking they had been given the location of some buried treasure. Ann explained to Susanna that a man called Roger Pyewall had once lived in her house and had been told to dig in the garden by visiting spirits. Roger, not made of such stern stuff as the women, refused and had since died.

Ann Taylor was not only a pragmatist, she was a woman who cheerfully allowed self-interest to come before friendship. She told the Swappers the treasure was rightfully hers and generously offered them £100 for finding out exactly where the treasure was. Presumably, they didn't go too deeply into her claim and obligingly checked with their resident ghosts. The spirits said the money was indeed buried in the garden, but sent Susanna on a curious journey to a place called Weeks Green where she saw strange figures and crocks of gold.

All this might seem ridiculous now, but the tale was taken seriously enough then. Ann and Susanna were arrested for consulting evil spirits and thrown in gaol. At the Rye General Session, they were tried, found guilty and condemned to death.

That might well have been the last anyone heard of Ann and Susanna, but Ann's husband George appealed to higher authorities and secured a stay of execution. During the enquiries, the name Martha Higgons came to light. Martha was the wife of the Mayor who had tried the case and it seemed she held a grudge against Ann and had influenced the court. Ann obviously didn't care for Martha either. She had accused her of consorting with her first husband, Thomas Hamon, before their marriage and commented on the fact that Martha had married her second husband with unseemly haste, only three weeks after the death of her first. Martha had retaliated by giving evidence in court accusing Ann of bewitching Hamon to death. Mayor Higgons, caught in the cross-fire, refused to release Ann on bail and George Taylor appealed to the Lord Warden of the Cinque Ports saying Ann was pregnant and 'grown very weak by reason thereof and the loathsomeness of the prison'. Reluctantly, Higgons finally backed down and Ann was released on bail of £100. The case wasn't finally sorted out until almost four years later when Ann and Susanna were cleared of all charges, thanks to legal advisers at Rye who decided their case was covered by the general pardon. Although it had taken a good few years, Ann Taylor and Susanna Swapper at last experienced the good fortune of the many other Sussex witches who escaped execution. Unfortunately for them, they weren't quite so lucky as treasure hunters. ❏

NAN TUCK
(c.l7th century)
A GHOSTLY TALE

How best to describe the story of Nan Tuck, fact or fable? When did she live and where? Was she an old crone or a beautiful young woman, a witch or a murderess?

One thing we can be sure of is that she was once thought sufficiently real to have a lane named after her. The most frequently told story says Nan was an old woman from Rotherfield who poisoned her husband. No one seems to know why she murdered him, but her crime was soon discovered. She fled from her home with her neighbours in chase. In fear of her life, she ran towards Buxted turning this way and that, but never quite managing to throw off her pursuers. As they caught up with her at last, in a lane not far from the village, she disappeared into some trees. They dived after her in a second, but although they searched every inch of the woods, not a single trace of her could they find. Nan Tuck had disappeared.

Another version of the tale has Nan accused of witchcraft and fleeing from a gang of locals intent on ducking her in the mill pond to see if she could prove her innocence by drowning. In desperation, she made for the church in the hope of claiming sanctuary. Some say the mob chased her into the woods before she could get there, others that she reached the doors only to be turned away by the vicar who refused her sanctuary because she was a witch. Whichever happened, her body was found hanging in the woods. Had she killed herself or had the local people found a more convenient way of ridding their village of a woman they saw as a threat?

Some accounts say the events described happened in the 17th century, others that they happened as much as two centuries later. The date is as lost as the lady herself Whoever Nan Tuck was, she is buried, they say, in an unsanctified grave under a stone slab outside the church wall. But that isn't where her story ends.

Not very many years ago, a young couple were strolling along the lane one evening, intent on each other as only lovers can be, when an apparition rose out of the darkness in front of them. Terrified, the girl screamed and took to her heels leaving her lover standing in the road. Although her home was several miles away, she didn't stop until she had reached its safety. Afterwards, neither of them could describe exactly what they had seen, but both were sure it had been the ghost of Nan Tuck and nothing ever convinced them otherwise.

Walking along Nan Tuck's Lane today, it is easy to imagine a dark night and her ghost endlessly running to escape her pursuers. You can almost hear her cries as she tries to flee into the trees. And if you search hard enough, it is said you can find a place where no vegetation will grow, a place deep in the woods that marks the spot where Nan Tuck last stood alive. ❑

JULIE TULLIS
(1939 – 1986)

"I DO NOT MIND LIVING DANGEROUSLY".
by Chris McCooey

In her autobiography Clouds from Both Sides, Julie Tullis cites her very European background as the basic reason for her wanderlust which took her to mountain areas all over the world. Her father, Francis (always known as 'Paco'), was Spanish and Erica, her mother, was German Swiss – and further back there were French ancestors, one of whom was the personal dentist to the Imperial Family of Russia and often travelled to St Petersburg to peer into Romanov mouths.

Her parents were in the restaurant business and met and married in a place which was the very antithesis of a wild and remote area – Selsdon, Surrey. It was here that Julie was born six months before the outbreak of the Second World War. Right from the start she seems not to have been cut out for a conventional upbringing; she and her elder sister, Zita, were always getting into scrapes.

Evacuated to a boarding school in Cambridge during the war, Julie had the distinction of being expelled (and sent back to the bombs of London) at the tender age of four. Part of the reason for the expulsion was the school having to call out the local doctor during the black-out, to extricate a number of rubber buttons that Julie had bitten off her night-dress and had pushed up her nose for a dare.

Even as a child, Julie appears to have had little fear of heights. The two girls used to climb out onto the roof of the house where they lived in London and have midnight feasts 60 feet above the ground.

The first time she climbed on rock was in 1954 when she went with her sister's climbing club to North Wales to make up the numbers – right from the start she was hooked and realised that climbing and mountains were for her.

Julie's mother used to take the girls on a holiday each summer – she would buy an old banger, load it with camping gear and take off to visit family in Germany and Switzerland. On these trips they would make a point of driving into the mountains of France, Italy and Austria as well.

Leaving school at 17, Julie got a job in a motor showroom in the Gloucester Road in London and began saving threepenny bits from her £5-a-week salary in a whisky bottle. By October 1956, she had saved enough (2,400 coins – which did not please the bank clerk) for the deposit on a Vespa scooter. This allowed her to get away every weekend to go climbing. It became a regular feature of her life to drive out of London to the High Rocks, a sandstone outcrop just outside Tunbridge Wells, and it was here she met her husband-to-be, Terry. They married in 1959.

Two years later, Terry was asked to run an Outdoor Pursuits Centre just a few miles into Sussex from Tunbridge Wells at Bowles Rock. Their first home after leaving their London flat was a large chicken shed by a stream, but both enjoyed the unsophisticated lifestyle and loved living in the country.

The couple earned enough from teaching rock climbing and selling climbing equipment. Children came along – Christopher and Lindsay – and they took over the village store in Groombridge and added a cafe as well. Terry was appointed the warden of Harrison Rocks, yet another sandstone outcrop nearby, and their lives jogged along – it was a fairly hand-to-mouth existence, but they were getting a good reputation for teaching 'difficult' school children and those who were handicapped.

At this time, Julie began to study martial arts – aikido and karate – and found that the training was complementary to that needed for rock climbing. She wrote: "They both bring body and mind into harmony . . . so that the energy flows out through the limbs. You can be shown the way but most of the discovery you must do for yourself"

She was often asked to take groups of would-be climbers to North Wales and, on one of these trips in 1976, her life changed immeasurably. It was an experience that in the next ten years would lead her into a new world of high altitude mountaineering and make her one of the most expert and respected mountaineers of the 20th century. Invariably the only female, she teamed up with noted Austrian film-maker, Kurt Diemberger to make the film record of several major expeditions – with Kurt, she was part of the 'highest film crew' in the world as they often spent weeks above 8,000m.

But that is jumping ahead. Back in 1976, in North Wales, one of Britain's finest rock climbers invited Julie – competent, but not expert – to make some climbs with him. Alec Sharp showed Julie how to climb naturally, without conscious effort. She wrote: "One of the pleasures I get from climbing is watching someone moving smoothly and competently on rock; it is a form of vertical ballet and visually very aesthetic."

From that time, she realised her martial arts training had extended into her climbing, bringing a totally new freedom. This natural high is what all climbers strive for – and climbing with Alec on that day, Julie experienced it for the first time. She wrote in her diary: "I was ready for any voyage into the unknown now."

In 1978, she and Terry went on an expedition to Peru. Terry could not tackle the highest peaks as he had suffered a bad accident when a garden rotavator went out of control and a spike had gone right through his leg. But Julie was fit and strong enough to get to the top of a number of mountains and even scaled Peru's highest peak, Huascaran (6,768m), with Norman Croucher – a climber with not one, but two, artificial legs.

With the children grown up, Julie had more and more time to devote to climbing. In 1980, she had been given a camera by Terry before setting off to climb in Yosemite in the United States and found she had a facility for taking good photos, not just pretty pictures. She began to illustrate her lectures with her own slides and helped other climbers arrange lecture tours in the UK. Following such a tour by Kurt Diemberger, the Austrian asked her to go with him as his assistant to film a French expedition in the summer of 1982 – it intended to climb the eighth highest peak in the world – Nanga Parbat (8, 126m), in Pakistan.

The two complemented each other in their high altitude work – both were orderly and careful when it came to climbing and film making. The expedition was successful in that a German climber, in a solo effort, got to the top of the mountain, but there was considerable tension among the other climbers. Julie, as the only woman, found it a particularly hard apprenticeship into international expeditions and high altitude film making.

In 1983, Julie and Kurt were back in the Himalayas again this time to film an Italian expedition which was hoping to climb K2 – at 8611m the world's second highest peak – from the Chinese side. For this expedition, Julie had learned Italian and taught herself to play the guitar to add to the conviviality of life in base camp. By now, she was looking forward to these times in wild and remote places – it was a kind of communion for her in which she left the outside world for the true world of nature.

When exploring in the footsteps of the great names from earlier days – Sir Francis Younghusband, Eric Shipton, H W Tilman – she wrote: "I felt completely in harmony with my surroundings. It was like looking at and being part of a great work of art. Mountains offer the ultimate human experience – to be involved physically, mentally and spiritually . . . the joy of being in such a situation was overwhelming."

Like most climbers, Julie was fatalistic. In her autobiography, she writes: "Some dangers you can avoid with your own skills, others are fate? luck? chance? all things over which you have absolutely no control, although your reaction at the time can have a strong bearing on the outcome."

The statistics tell their own story. One in 12 Himalayan mountaineers dies in the mountains. Julie wrote, prophetically as it turned out: "If I could choose a place to die, it would be in the mountains." Already she had had a number of narrow escapes – sliding out of control down a mountain towards a precipice, but managing to stop just in time, and being caught in avalanches. She knew how seductive tiredness in mountains could be, when you were at the limit of your mental and physical abilities. "There have been a number of occasions in the mountains, when just to sit still and drift into an eternal sleep would have been an easy and pleasant thing to do, but hopefully the circle of nature will not close for me too soon. I have a lot to live for."

It was not to be. In 1983, Julie had got to 8,000m on K2 – the highest a British woman had ever climbed. In 1984, she was back on the mountain again, filming for British television an attempt from the Pakistani side by a Swiss expedition. While on this expedition, she climbed to the top of her first 8,000m mountain – Broad Peak (8047m) – with Kurt. She was the first British woman to stand on the summit. The following year, she was back again but this time filming an expedition attempting to climb Chomolungma – the Mother Goddess of the World – otherwise known as Everest (8,848m). And she tried again to climb Nanga Parbat, but had to turn back at 7,600m.

Over Christmas 1985, Julie was on her travels with Terry, for a change, in America. Her husband had always been supportive of his wife and never stood in her way as she went off for months on end in the company of other men. As Julie wrote in her book about sharing tents in the mountains: "Sex is one of the last things that you think about." Many mountaineers will tell you that the euphoria (even the ecstasy) comes from the natural high of being in high places – for them it is heaven on earth and better than sex.

In March 1986, they parted for the last time. Terry was going to help on a school skiing trip and Julie was going back to film yet another expedition on K2. To the climbing fraternity, K2 is known as the mountain of mountains. Up to 1985, only eight expeditions (one in every seven attempts) had succeeded in climbing the peak and less than 20 climbers had ever stood on the top compared with more than 100 who had conquered Everest,

In June of that year, there were ten groups – 60 climbers in total – in the base camp. By the end of the climbing season, a fifth of them would be dead.

Julie made one attempt at the summit, but had to turn back when only 300m from the top. By this time, six climbers had already died on the mountain – in falls or swept away by avalanches. She wrote to Terry after her unsuccessful attempt: "To get three hours from the top and go down safely, means more to me than standing on the summit. I have no more pleasure to climb the mountain of mountains."

The weather was not helping either, but at the beginning of August it improved. A group of Koreans and Poles decided to have one last go at the summit – they made it, but one of the Poles fell to his death on the way down. A second group of seven, including Julie and Kurt and the English climber, Alan Rouse, also decided to give it one last effort. Despite deteriorating weather, Kurt and Julie, who were roped together as usual, made it and stood on the summit of their dreams. But there was drama to come – on the way down they slipped and were swept towards a drop of 3,000m. Both thought they were going to die, but they came to a stop just before the abyss. Then darkness overtook them and they were forced to spend an endless night in a snow hole.

The next day, August 5th, the whole group made it down to tents at 8,000m but the weather closed in and they were forced to shelter. The storm was ferocious; the wind unrelenting. They could not move. Dehydration, frost-bite and hypothermia began to take hold as the supplies of food and cooking gas ran out. Julie died on August 7th.

The storm finally blew itself out on August 10th. Alan Rouse was too weak to leave the tents and was left. Two Austrians made it out of the tent, but collapsed soon after starting the descent. A Polish woman tried as well but disappeared on the way down. Only Kurt and a German climber got off the mountain alive.

128

On September 27th 1986, Terry held a 'remembrance' for Julie at the High Rocks. It was attended by 500 people. As well as her family and friends, there were climbers from all over the world including Kurt Diemberger, who had lost a number of fingers and toes. to frost-bite but apart from that had recovered from his ordeal. Members of the local martial arts club performed a 'musogi' – a cleansing ceremony – to help express and purify their collective grief

At the end of Clouds from Both Sides, Julie had written: 'Only those who risk going too far can possibly find out how far they can go.

Julie's body remains in her last resting place on K2. ❏

SARAH, COUNTESS OF WALDEGRAVE
(1787 – 1873)

HASTINGS' AUTOCRATIC BENEFACTOR ,
by Norma Batley

Sarah was born in 1787 in the Hastings Old Town Rectory, the younger daughter of the Reverend William Whitear. It is probable that, according to the custom of the day, she and her sister would have been taught at home by a governess, What is certain is that she was brought up in the faith of the Anglican Church and this faith profoundly affected, and indeed guided, her life and actions. To this strong Christian conviction was added the influence of her first husband, Edward Milward (Junior) whom she married when she was 30.

Both Edward Milward (Senior) – Sarah's father-in-law – and her husband had been Mayor of Hastings and were public spirited men. From her husband, Sarah would have learned about the affairs of the town but also, significantly, after Edward's death in 1837, she inherited a lifetime's interest in the Milward estates. At the age of 48, Sarah came into possession of very considerable wealth, land and property.

All her life Sarah had had a certain 'social standing'. But her second marriage to William, 8th Earl of Waldegrave made her , a distinguished member of the aristocracy.

During Sarah's lifetime, the town of Hastings was going through a period of exceptionally rapid growth. The railway line to London and the building of St Leonards brought great changes. The small town, known to every school child as the place that gave its name to the battle between King Harold and William the Conqueror, began to become established as a popular seaside resort. The population grew from 6,300 in 1821 to 29,291 in 1871.

The obituary notice in the *Hastings and St Leonards News* of April 25th 1873, records that as Mrs Milward, and later as the Countess Waldegrave, Sarah laid the foundation stones of no less than seven Hastings churches . . . but only after she had carefully scrutiised the building plans. Financial support – usually ranging from £500 to £1,000 – and sometimes the donation of land and furnishing for the interiors were also given. In one case, the stone for the entire church was paid for by her.

Typically comment and advice were offered at the same time. Sarah was never slow to come forward with a speech on the ceremonial occasions and frequently she would take the opportunity to voice her opinion and her abhorrence of any tendency towards the recent introduction of 'ritualistic practices' in the Church. On one such occasion, a clergyman standing by was heard to exclaim: "Her ladyship should have been a Bishop."

If the support of the Anglican Church was her first consideration, schools for the poor were another. Sarah was responsible for one of the first Sunday Schools in the country and she was one of the prime movers in establishing schools for the education of both boys and girls in the Old Town. Following meetings of the Hastings Parochial School Society established in 1835 for 'the education of the poor', plans developed and it was Sarah who provided a house (previously owned by the Milwards) for use as a school. As ever, Sarah made suggestions regarding this project and it was at her insistence that the school was to be maintained by voluntary subscription and partly by small sums from the scholars. There were to be separate entrances for 'Boys' and 'Girls' and 'if ever the boys were permitted to enter from Tackleway (the girls' entrance) her gift would be void and she might take back the property'

Her husband William, Earl Waldegrave, was a member of the Schools' Council. Described as 'a congenial partner' he 'heartily assisted her in benevolent and pious works' and is said to have endeared himself to the townspeople. Later, at a time when the need for increasing the facilities became urgent, Sarah wrote to the chairman of the Council: "Lord Waldegrave and myself have been very anxiously considering the absolute necessity there is for an additional Boys School." The suggestion was made to move the girls elsewhere. The letter continued: "I hope you will excuse me from making a condition on the present occasion, which is that I shall be most happy to bestow £500 for the purpose of erecting a girls' schoolroom, providing that I approve of the place, plans, etc, etc, and I shall indeed rejoice to hear the work is likely to be completed."

While provision of churches and schools were Sarah's priorities, there is no doubt that the building of Waldegrave Public Baths and Wash Houses in the middle of the Old Town would have been, in the opinion of some inhabitants, the most popular development of all. Many of the cottages and dwellings in the Old Town had meagre, if any, washing facilities and these new buildings were much used. A secondary benefit, which may not have been foreseen, was that by taking in washing, women could earn a little extra money to help make ends meet. The wash houses were only demolished in 1960 and are still talked about today.

Among other concerns at that time was the state of the local Rifle Corps. In the mid 19th century, there were still fears of a possible invasion from France. When Sarah's attention was drawn to this, her response was magnanimous – £250 was given for the men's clothing, arrangements were made for a drill ground and land was offered on Sarah's estates for use as a rifle range. Captain Rock bore public testimony 'to the debt which the Rifle Corps owed to her Ladyship.' Once Sarah was convinced of a need and had sympathy with it, it was said 'her purse was as ready as her influence.'

The last benefaction that the Countess gave was a building in the Old Town for the use of the town's fishermen. Once more she was concerned with the spiritual as well as physical welfare of others. She wanted the institution to be 'a resort in business hours for the Fishermen' but also she hoped that it would 'exercise a decided religious and moral influence for good.'

And what of Sarah herself? From a portrait of her as a young woman that hangs in her old home – The Mansion – (now Old Hastings House) she appears to have an alert and serious expression with features neither noticeably pretty nor plain. As an old lady, her expression had hardened. From her step-granddaughter, we have an account of the house and the old lady in her last years. In Lady Riddings' unpublished memoirs she states: 'Grandmama was patron of all the livings in and around Hastings.

She ruled the church with a rod of iron and any papacy or papistical leanings had scant money from her.'

This account continues with a description of certain weeks in the year given up to the household laundry. 'The footman did nothing but turn the mangle. Nobody was allowed proper meals or fires – the drains needed overhauling, but Grandmama refused, counting it "'newfangled nonsense to have such notions." Grandmama had grown very cranky and queer' . Clearly she did not spend money on home comforts for herself or servants.

Now, a century and a half later, it would be easy to criticise, but Sarah was a product of the times she lived in, and she did what she believed to be her Christian duty in Victorian England.

All the churches she patronised (except one) are still functioning; the modern successors to her schools still serve the town and the Fishermen's Institute flourishes, albeit with the addition of something she may well not have approved of – a licence to sell and consume alcohol.

The label attached to the ceremonial silver trowel used by Sarah on many occasions reads: 'Sarah, Countess of Waldegrave, a generous though autocratic benefactor' .

The last word must be left with the people of Hastings who actually knew her and were moved to erect a drinking fountain in the centre of the town, 12 years before she died. The inscription reads:

SARAH
COUNTESS OF WALDEGRAVE

'In recognition of the constant support afforded by her to the religious and benevolent institutions of the Borough and the neighbourhood. The money for this fountain was collected by Public Subscription by the inhabitants of Hastings and St Leonards including the pence of children and young persons educated in the National Schools.' ❑

MARY WHEATLAND
(1835-1924)

BOGNOR'S LIFE SAVER

S he was called the Grace Darling of the South. In her life, she saved over 30 people from drowning and became one of Bognor's most celebrated characters.

Mary was born in Aldingbourne in 1835, then just a small village to the east of Chichester. At the age of 14, she came to Bognor and went to work for a woman called Mrs Mills who operated bathing machines on the beach. She took to her new life with enthusiasm, learnt to dive and often spent an hour and a half swimming without rest – no light task when you remember the all-concealing, serge costumes of the day.

In 1857, she married George Wheatland and began producing a large family. When they moved to South Bersted on the outskirts of Bognor, Mary was already known for her life-saving exploits. The local vicar published details of 13 rescues in the Bersted parish magazine. First was the overweight wife of a London brewer 'whose soul was drifting into eternity and her body across the Channel'.

134

Second was a nurse and third was a little French lady whose cries were heard as she floated towards the horizon. The sea was heavy that day, but Mary swam to the rescue, caught hold of her dress and towed her to safety. Mary hadn't reached the stage of self-employment by then and when the foreign lady asked the owner of the bathing machines how she might reward Mary, she was told "she needn't give her anything".

She wasn't always so unfortunate. One woman she saved rewarded her with the princely sum of threepence, but an elderly gentleman was more generous after being plucked from the sea and gave her £20.

One man Mary saved – number seven in the vicar of Bersted's list – got in such a state of panic that he grabbed Mary in a 'wild grasp' and would have drowned her too if she hadn't anchored herself to a groyne.

She didn't confine herself to single rescues. On one occasion she rescued six young girls who were, as one onlooker said, "all drowning in a batch". The girls were in high spirits and had gone out of their depth. Mary swam round behind them and brought them in one at a time. When Mary was asked about the incident, she said, "Pray don't say anything about it, for they were very good to me: they gave me £2 towards back rent, and sent me a bit of beef at Christmas."

Mary gained national recognition when she was featured in the Illustrated London News in 1879 and in the same year was awarded an Honorary Testimonial by the Royal Humane Society. Her modest response was that she considered 'the saving of life to be as much the work of a bathing woman as the rinsing of a bathing dress.'

Life wasn't easy. George died in 1881 and Mary continued to work as she struggled to bring up her six children. She taught holiday-makers to swim and was employed by local private boarding schools to teach their girls. By this time, she was mistress of her own bathing machines and was loved for her kindness, her courage and her unfailing energy.

When she was 71, she gave up diving off the pier and standing on her head in the sea waving her legs in the air, saying she thought she was "getting a bit old for that kind of thing." She had never believed in drying herself after swimming, convinced no one ever caught a cold from sea-water and perhaps she paid the price when old age brought with it rheumatism.

Postcards were issued in her honour showing her proudly wearing her medals. In 1903, six years before she officially retired, the town of Bognor arranged a benefit for her. Among the guests were Princess Alice and her husband, the Duke of Teck. Mary Wheatland was 89 when she died in 1924. Her coffin was carried to Bersted graveyard by the local fishermen who had known her all their lives and who would miss her for the rest of their own. ❏

BARBARA WILLARD
(1909-1994)

FRIEND OF THE FOREST

Sussex has always attracted writers. Many have visited here and remembered it in their work and others have taken the county to their hearts and settled here. Others still were born here and have remained faithful all their lives. Barbara Willard was one of these.

Born in Brighton on March 12th 1909, she lived the greater part of her long life in Sussex. She was a modest lady of great dignity and a prolific and prize-winning author. She was also a tireless fighter for the preservation of Ashdown Forest, an area unique in England and one which has been constantly threatened over the centuries.

Barbara had a spell treading the boards when she was young, which was hardly surprising as her great-uncle, her father, brother and cousins were all actors. But she had begun to make up stories long before this. By the age of seven, she had already realised writing was where her real ambitions lay.

She finished her first novel not long after leaving school and was soon working in Mudie's lending library in London. In her spare time, she continued to develop her craft and wrote more novels, the first of which was published when she was 22. She went on to write for several film companies, among them MGM and Twentieth Century Fox, and later became a reader for a literary agent.

Ashdown Forest had always been one of her favourite haunts. Barbara and her family were living in Richmond when the Second World War was declared and on the following Sunday they went down to the forest for a picnic. She described it later as a magical day. While she was sitting quietly, a sudden rustling came from the undergrowth and a young deer wearing a bell leapt past and disappeared again. Deer roam the forest freely, but the sight and sound affected Barbara deeply. She said she felt as if her heart stopped in wonder during those few seconds.

After the war, she left Richmond and returned to Sussex, living with her great friend the journalist and photographer, Frances Howell, in the village of Kingston. Barbara always referred to herself as a writer. On one occasion, when she and Frances were travelling in Norway, Barbara was asked what was the difference between a writer and a journalist. With dry humour and a sideways glance at Frances, Barbara answered, "I *know* that I'm writing fiction."

In Kingston, she got to know many of the local children and it was then that she first thought about writing for young people. Although Kingston would still seem like a quiet village to many of us, it gradually grew over the years and eventually Barbara decided to move on. The solitude and her happy memories made Ashdown Forest the obvious place for her to live. She and Frances bought an 18th century cottage, complete with the Commoner s right to collect fodder and firewood from the forest and Barbara fell in love with the area all over again.

Almost immediately, she began gathering the stories and records which she would one day use in her book about Ashdown, although it was ten years before she felt she had absorbed the forest into her blood sufficiently to use the setting in a novel. Reading any of her series of eight Mantlemass novels now, you could almost be forgiven for thinking they were written by the forest itself In 1974, having been runner-up twice before with other books, Barbara won the Guardian Award for Children s Fiction with *The Iron Lily*. Another of her books with a forest setting, *The Queen of the Pharisees' Children*, won the 1983 Whitbread Award.

For many years, Barbara served on the Ashdown Forest Board of Conservators and there was probably no one better qualified to write about the area. In her book, *The Forest – Ashdown in East Sussex*, she traced the history of the land from primeval times to the present, apologising at the outset for the amount of material she was forced to leave out. Her own words described the book as a modest volume, but this was a reflection of the lady herself, not of her work. Tales are told of 13th century royalty who selfishly guarded their hunting grounds, of Commoners who fought to maintain their rights and of the Conservators who continue the fight. She painted a picture of a harsh land which survived despite the threat of clearance, enclosure and commercialism. A land which allowed its people a living, but which took a toll on their lives. She wrote about the animals, the trees and plants and she wrote about the ghosts – like those remembered by visitors to The Airman's Grave, a monument to the pilot and crew of the Wellington bomber that limped back from a raid on Cologne in 1941, but which crashed on the forest before it could reach home. Reading her book about Ashdown brings tears as well as laughter and above all the knowledge that the story was told with love. Barbara said simply, "It was a book I had to write."

If you stand looking across the ragged landscape of gorse ridges to the wooded glens and tall clumps of pine, it takes little imagination to understand why she felt the need to write about Ashdown Forest. But only an exceptional writer could attempt such a book and actually bring the forest alive off the page. Barbara Willard succeeded.

I was fortunate enough to meet her shortly before she died in February, 1994. She showed me into her study and sat at her desk in front of the window looking out onto her garden where the standard poodle, Chokki, played with Jemmy, the Yorkshire Terrier. Beyond was the forest where her characters had come to life. During the interview, she gave me the distinct impression that if I was going to write about her, she would make very sure that I did a good job. Later, Frances told me that when the draft of The Forest – Ashdown in East Sussex was finished, Barbara had given her the job of completing the incredibly complex index in just two weeks. Frances succeeded in her task. I hope I succeeded in mine. I think I did – when I went back to pick up the copy of my article which Barbara had insisted on checking before it went to print, she was still being extremely nice to me, Even on such a short acquaintance, I realised that if Barbara expected a lot of those around her, she was willing to give all that she could in return. I can still remember her very clearly sitting in her study, the colourful jackets of her many books looking cheerfully down from the book-shelves. No doubt she will be remembered mostly for the wonderfully rich stories of her Mantlemass novels, and I'm sure that is the way she would want to be remembered. But for me, the book that stood out on her shelves most vividly was the one which was closest to her heart: *The Forest – Ashdown in East Sussex.* ❏

FRANCES GARNET, VISCOUNTESS WOLSELEY

FOUNDER OF GLYNDE COLLEGE FOR LADYGARDENERS

Frances Garnet Wolseley wasn't born in Sussex, but there have been few women who have been closer to this county or who have loved it more. She was, in fact, born in Dublin. The year was 1872 and her parents were Field Marshal Viscount Wolseley and his wife, Louisa. By the time Frances was ten years old, her father's name had become a household word. Among many other victories, his success in the Ashanti wars and the Egyptian campaign had made him famous. When people wanted to say everything would be all right, they would say it would be, "All Sir Garnet." The Viscount was the 'model of a modern Major-General'.

Already nearing 40 when his only child was born, the Viscount spent at least half of his time abroad and Louisa and Frances led an army life. Her father's ADCs nicknamed Frances 'Pusskins' . She and her mother were always on the move. There were long periods of separation combined with intervals of frantic social activity. Louisa's talent for home-making was put to good use and it was from her that Frances inherited a love of gardening. Through her parents, Frances met the likes of Lord Tennyson and Andrew Lang, and as a child, she visited Windsor and later wrote about Queen Victoria in her diary.

She was presented at Court in 1891. Her natural good-humour made her popular and her laughter was never far away. She loved to dance and took part in the round of balls and house parties in many country houses – she knew George V and taught his brother, Prince Eddy, to dance the Washington Post. But she was always a country girl and she loved riding to hounds and long country walks with her dogs. She and Louisa became friendly with Charles Kempe who was then in his early fifties and famous for his stained glass, and they often visited him at his home in Lindfleld. He talked to her endlessly of country life and country lore and increased her knowledge of gardening and garden design, introducing her to many of his gardening friends. No doubt it was with Kempe that Frances first went to William Robinson's garden at Gravetye which became one of her haunts and it was during such visits that her love for Sussex began to eclipse her lively interest in other places.

In 1898, when the Viscount's military career was coming to an end, he and Louisa moved to Farm House at Glynde, an old house shadowed by Mount Caburn and looking out over the meanderings of the Ouse River to the Downs and the Channel at Newhaven. Frances loved it there. She had become an independent young woman – often irritating her parents who would have preferred her to remain under their influence as the perfect, dutiful daughter. She deplored an idle life and wanted to do something practical. The Suffrage Movement was yet to come, but Frances was well aware of the difficulties faced by women in the late 19th century and realised the need for socially acceptable employment. She began passing on her knowledge of smallholding management and food production, employing women gardeners at Farm House and training them in general horticulture.

Eventually, she bought some land on the unpromising chalk slopes of Mount Caburn around the house called 'Ragged Lands' and extended her dream by opening the Glynde College for Lady Gardeners.

The term 'lady gardeners' makes you think of half an hour between coffee and cocktails spent deadheading roses, but Frances wasn't interested in teaching her students the polite graces, she wanted to produce professional gardeners and growers who would leave her school with the qualifications to earn themselves a good living wage. The courses lasted a full two years, demanding total commitment, and Frances, being her father's daughter, organised them with military precision. She picked all the students herself, looking for spirit, intelligence and talent and often finding them in the daughters of officers in the forces. On the prospectus, her patrons' names included Gertrude Jekyll, William Robinson and Mrs Earle, sister of Countess Lytton.

The chalk slopes of Ragged Lands were south-facing, but completely unsheltered. Frances terraced them and planted hedges. She installed Elsa More, one of her first successful students, as Captain of the college and designed uniforms for the women that would have seemed quite unladylike at the time – mid-calf length skirts for walking out and short skirts over breeches with gaiters and boots for working. She was a hard taskmaster, but she saw no point in helping women to gain their independence if they didn't enjoy themselves at the same time and she often arranged moonlight lectures and picnics for her students. Her first book, *Gardening for Women*, was published in 1908 and she is probably better known as an author than for her innovative approach to gardening – although her writing obviously drew attention to the college. Her natural curiosity continually fuelled her interest in anything and everything to do with Sussex and her situation allowed her almost universal access – she wrote over 100 fascinating articles on old Sussex houses, great and small, for the *Sussex County Magazine*. And, of course, she wrote continually about gardens and gardening.

In 1913, she was given the freedom of the City of London at the suggestion of the Worshipful Company of Gardeners and in the same year her father died and she succeeded to the title of Viscountess. When the war came, she saw people leaving the countryside to work in armament factories and she realised there was an even greater need for women who could work the land productively. She wrote articles for *Nineteenth Century* and the *Contemporary Review*, and then a second book, *Women and the Land*, in which she said that food alone would give vigour and warmth to the soldiers and would keep up the spirits of the sailors who guarded our shores. In 1914, she founded a co-operative society called the Glynde District Federation of Growers and during the course of the war, she worked for the Board of Agriculture.

The college was closed not long after the war – Elsa More had died tragically young and Frances' mother died in 1920. Frances moved on, continuing her teaching work at Massetts Place, Scaynes Hill, as well as travelling, lecturing and writing. Her last home was Culpepers at Ardingly where she lived for the last 12 years of her life. There she turned the bare field around the house into one of the loveliest gardens in Sussex. Frances died on Christmas Eve 1936. She had been ill for some time and was very frail and losing her sight, but her curiosity and interest in life never left her. She continued writing and when she could no longer go out, she carried on her productive life, even if only within herself "I am so happy," she was moved to say just before she died. '1 have so much in my mind!" ❏

ILLUSTRATIONS

Dame Margery Corbett Ashby. The picture of Dame Margery Corbett Ashby is the property of The Observer and was previously reproduced by the Danehill Parish Historical Society in their booklet *From the Feudal to the JetAge.* We also thank Mrs Hylda Rawlings and Dr Michael Ashby FRCP

Michael Fairless Barber on her deathbed

Lady Anne Blunt in Arab dress and Judith Blunt, Lady Wentworth, portrait by her husband , the Hon. Neville Lytton, *Country Life,* September 14th 1978

Barbara Bodichon (line drawing by Susi)

Cornelia Connelly, about the time of her marriage, aged 22, in nun's habit (c. 1877). The Society of the Holy Child Jesus, Mayfield

Marie Corbett, Mrs Hylda Rawlings and Dr Michael Ashby, FRCP

Milly Dayrell, Eileen Burrough and David Burrough

Christiana Edmunds (line drawing by Susi)

Sarah Ann French, Rosalind Hodge

Gundrada, St John the Baptist Church, Southover, Lewes. (Chris McCooey)

Martha Gunn, *Sussex Lift, March 1971.* The original hangs in Buckingham Palace

Phoebe Hessell – aged 106

Sophia Jex-Blake – as a young woman. From a crayon drawing by Robert B. MeNeill

Sheila Kaye-Smith, Sheila Kaye-Smith Society

Dame Grace Kiminins, Chailey Heritage

Charlotte King in Greek play, Stonelands, 1910 – 1911 (Jasper Ridley)

Lawrence Sisters. Left to right: Dorothy, Penelope, Millicent. Roedean School

Vivien, Duchess of Leinster, with 83-year old Duke outside House of Lords, 1975. (Popperfoto)

Saint Lewinna, by permission of Beckett Newspapers

Lee Miller – self-portrait, New York, 1932. Penrose Film Productions Ltd

North End House Home School: Miss Edith – Back row, 5th from left; Miss Mary – Back row, 5th from right; Miss Knowles – 3rd from right. (Josephine Ferguson)

Joan, Lady Pelham (line drawing by Susi)

Vera G. Pragnell, by permission of Beckett Newspapers

Nancy Price

Mabel Raymonde-Hawkins, MBE, (Amanda Wilkins and The Raystede Centre for Animal Welfare)

Charlotte Smith, by permission of West Sussex Record Office

Susanna Stacey (line drawing by Susi)

Mrs Steere and Miss Rickman. Grave digger – Mrs Steere
    Miss Rickman's burial mound for her horse, Charlie, in Lewes (no longer in existence) by permission of Beckett Newspapers

Susanna Swapper and Ann Taylor (line drawing by Susi)

Nan Tuck, Chris McCooey

Julie Tullis – meditating in Monument Valley, USA. (Terry Tullis – Soft Rock)

Sarah, Countess of Waldegrave, Hastings Museum and Art Gallery

Mary Wheatland, from an old postcard

Barbara Willard (Frances Howell)

Frances Garnet, Viscountess Wolseley (line drawing by Susi)

For line drawings by Susi contact:

Susi Nightingale, Box and Rose Cottage, Capton, Dartmouth, Devon TQ6 0JE

Tel: 01803 712579

SOURCES AND FURTHER READING

1. **Dame Margery Corbett Ashby**
   Ashby, Dr Michael Corbett, *Dame Margery Corbett Ashby*, Danehill Parish Historical Society Magazine (November 1992)
   Danehill Parish Historical Society, *From the Feudal to the JetAge* (November 1982)

2. **Margaret Barber**
   Anderson, Arthur Henry, *The Roadmender's Country*, Southern Railway (1924)
   Fairless, Michael, *The Roadmender*, Duckworth

3. **Lady Anne Blunt and Judith Blunt, Lady Wentworth**
   Fitchew, Jean, *Riding World* in West Sussex County Times (June 13th 1986)
   Kendall, Ena, *Beautiful Horses – and a family feud* in Observer Magazine (January 23rd 1977)
   Little, Philip, *The Rescue of a Victorian Dream* in Crawley Observer (September 23rd 1982)

4. **Barbara Bodichon**
   Burton, H., Barbara Bodichon, *Landscape Painters* in Sussex Biographical Pamphlets (vol.4)

5. **Cornelia Connelly**
   Armour, Mary Andrew, *Cornelia*, Exposition Press (1979)
   Wadham, Juliana, *The Case of Cornelia Connelly*, Collins (1956)

6. **Marie Corbett**
   Davenport, Leonie, *The Union or Workhouse System of Poor Relief Post-1834* in Danehill Parish Historical Society Magazine (September 1987)
   Danehill Parish Historical Society, *From the Feudal to the JetAge* (November 1982)

7. **Christiana Edmunds**
   Walbrook, H. M., *The Poisoned Chocolates* in The Seaside Murders edited by Jonathan Goodman, Sphere (1987)

8. **Sarah Ann French**
   Beckett, Arthur, *The Onion Pie* in Sussex County Magazine (Vol.10)
   Taylor, Rupert, *Sussex Scandals,* Countryside Books (1987)

9. **Gundrada**
   Lower, Mark Antony, *The Worthies of Sussex*
   Anderson, Dr. Freda, *Uxor Mea: The First Wife of the First William of Warenne* in Sussex Archaeological Collections (vol.130)

10. **Martha Gunn**
    Niland, Diane, *Queen of 'em All* in Sussex Life (March 1971)

11. **Phoebe Hessel**
    Bedford, *S. M. Phoebe Hessel's* romantic story in Sussex Life (January 1973)
    Varney, Mary and MacKenzie, *Brighton's Amazon exposed* in Sussex Life (March 1988)

12. **Sophia Jex-Blake**
    Todd, Margaret, *The Life of Sophia Jex-Blake*

13. **Sheila Kaye-Smith**
    Kaye-Smith, Sheila., *The Children's Summer*, Cassell (1932)
    Selina Is Older, Cassell (1935)
    Joanna Godden, Virago (1973)
    Secretary, Sheila Kaye-Smith Soc.,
    Flat 2, Buckhurst Court, 29 Buckhurst Rd, Bexhill-on-Sea, East Sussex, TN4O 1QE

14. **Dame Grace Kimmins**
    Lawrie, Rose Mary, *The Heritage Craft Schools,* Chailey in Sussex County Magazine (Vol. 25)
    Ronald, Joan, *Chailey Heritage, Craft School and Hospital*

15. **Penelope, Dorothy And Millicent Lawrence**
    A History of Roedean School, The Founders of Roedean, Farncombe's (1935)

16. **Saint Lewinna**
    Blaauw, W. H., *On the Translation of Saint Lewinna from Seaford,* in 1058 in Sussex Archaeological Collections (Vol. 1)
    Povey, Kenneth, *Saint Lewinna, The Sussex Martyr* in Sussex County Magazine (Vol. 2)
    Whatmore, L. E., *St. Lewinna: East Sussex Martyr* (1979)

17. Lee Miller
Penrose, Antony, *The Lives of Lee Miller*, Thames and Hudson Ltd (1985)
Penrose, Antony, *Lee Miller's War*, Condé Nast Books (1992)
Penrose, Roland, *Scrap Book*, Thames and Hudson Ltd (1980)

18. North End House Home School
Dumbrell's School 1882-1982 (1982)

19. Joan, Lady Pelham
Fleet, Charles, *Glimpses of Our Sussex Ancestors*, Lewes, Farncombe and Co. (1882)
Pelham, Hon. Mrs Arthur and Mclean, David, *Some Early Pelhams*, Combridges

20. Vera G. Pragnell
Pragnell, Vera G, *The Story of the Sanctuary*, Steyning, The Vine Press

21. Nancy Price
Price, Nancy. *Into An Hour Glass*, Museum Press Ltd (1953)

22. Mabel Raymonde-Hawkins, Mbe
Sands, Sarah, *I Have a Dream* in My Weekly (February 5th 1994)
The Raystede Centre for Animal Welfare, Ringmer, East Sussex, BN8 5AJ

23. Charlotte Smith
Scott, Hardiman, *Secret Sussex*, Batchworth Press Ltd (1949)

24. Susanna Stacey
Woodward, Marcus, *Mistress of Stanton's Farm*, Heath Cranton Ltd

25. Susanna Swapper And Ann Taylor
Valiente, Doreen, *Where Witchcraft Lives*, Aquarian Press (1962)

26. Nan Tuck
Sivers, Dorothy E. M., *The Story of Nan Tuck: A Sussex Legend* in Sussex County Magazine (Vol.14)

27. Julie Tullis
Tullis, Julie, *Clouds From Both Sides*, Grafton Books (1986)

28. Countess Waldegrave
Baines, Mainwaring, *Historic Hastings*
Peake, Steve, *Fishermen of Hastings*

29. Mary Wheatland
Allaway, Jim, *Mary was the 'Grace Darling of the South'* in The Observer (May 28th 1976)
Mills, Vanessa, *Mary: A lifesaver extraordinary* in The Observer (April 19th 1990)
Price, Bernard, *People, Places and Things* in The Observer (April 29th 1977)

30. Barbara Willard
Willard, Barbara, *The Forest – Ashdown in East Sussex*, Sweethaws Press (1989)

31. Frances Garnet, Viscountess Wolseley
Brown, Jane, *Eminent Gardeners 1880-1980*

Other Publications Include:
Country Life; Crawley Observer; Evening Argus; The Macmillan Dictionary of Women's Biography; Magnet; The Mid-Sussex Times; West Sussex Gazette; Who Was Who.

General Reading
Beckett, Arthur, *The Wonderful Weald*
Mee, Arthur, *The Spirit of the Downs: Sussex*
Lucas, E. V., *Highways and Byways in Sussex*
Wymer, Norman, *Companion into Sussex*
Robertson, Charles A., *Hailsham And Its Environs*
Stuart, Elsie, *An Illustrated History of Pevensey*

Sharon Searle was born, literally, at the foot of the South Downs. Having lived all her life in Sussex, she cannot imagine wanting to live anywhere else.

She began writing at the age of 32 and had a number of short stories published and broadcast before turning to non-fiction. Her writings about people and places in Sussex appear regularly in print and a second book about Sussex women is in preparation.

Still within sight of the Downs, she now lives in Polegate with her husband and her Jack Russell terrier, Gyp.